CHOOSE THE BEST SELF-PUBLISHING SERVICES: ASSEMBLING YOUR TOOLS AND TEAM

JOHN DOPPLER

ALLIANCE OF INDEPENDENT AUTHORS

Series Editor
ORNA A. ROSS

CONTENTS

A Note about Pronouns   1
A Note about ALLi   2
A Note About ALLi's Watchdog Desk   5

PART I
INTRODUCTION

1. How to Read This Book   9
2. Defining Our Terms   11
3. Publishers Don't Ask For Payment   17
4. The Independent Author   19
5. Writer Beware   27
6. The Value of Control   36

PART II
THE SEVEN PROCESSES OF PUBLISHING

7. Writing Services   43
8. Editorial Services   47
9. Design Services   53
10. Production Services   61
11. Distribution Services   67
12. Marketing Services   77
13. Promotion Services   87
14. Publishing Rights Services   95

PART III
ASSISTED SELF-PUBLISHING

15. Packaged Services   107
16. Vanity Presses   115
17. Hybrid Presses   119

PART IV
ALLI'S SERVICE RATINGS

The Ratings   125

18. About ALLi's Service Ratings   127
19. The Ratings   129

PART V
**HOW TO EVALUATE SELF-PUBLISHING
SERVICES**

20. The Rating Process   175
21. Ten Questions To Ask A Self-Publishing Service   191
22. ALLi Code of Standards   197
23. Conclusion   204

THE END

MORE ADVICE & FEEDBACK

Self-publishing Advice Center   209
Free Book for You   211
Review Request   212

Acknowledgments   213
About the Author   215
About ALLi   217
Index   219

A NOTE ABOUT PRONOUNS

A NOTE ABOUT ALLI

ANote about ALLi: Foreword by Orna Ross

This book is all about you. Your writing and publishing ambitions. Your books and your readers. Your income and influence and impact as a self-publishing author. It is based on the work of the Alliance of Independent Authors (ALLi).

The name ALLi is pronounced "ally" (al-eye), as that's what our alliance aims to be: the self-publisher's ally. And it's spelt with a small i and big ALL because its members are like the three musketeers in Dumas's eponymous novel: all working for each individual (the "i" in our name) and each for the larger all.

My husband Philip and I launched the organization at the London Book Fair 2012 and it has quickly grown to be global, with thousands of members and advisors all over the world. Our mission is to foster excellence and ethics in self-publishing, through service to authors and through advocacy with creative industry representatives and author organizations in seven key English-speaking territories across the world: Australia, Canada, Europe, New Zealand, South Africa, United Kingdom and United States.

ALLi's work is fourfold:

. . .

• We *advise*, providing **best-practice information and education** through our Self-Publishing Advice Center, which offers a daily blog, weekly live streams and podcasts, and a bookstore of self-publishing guidebooks.

• We *monitor* the self-publishing sector through our **watchdog desk**, alerting authors to bad actors and predatory players and running an approved partner program.

• We *campaign* for the **advancement of indie authors** in the publishing and literary sectors (bookstores, libraries, literary events, prizes, grants, awards and other author organizations) globally, encouraging the provision of publishing and business skills for authors, and furthering the indie author cause.

• We *serve* our members through various **member tools and resources** including author forums, contract advice, sample agreements, contacts and networking, literary agency representation, and a member care desk.

Our real strength is our membership. When you join ALLi, you're not just joining an organization, but a movement. A chaotic, kaleidoscopic, liberating, exciting and self-organizing movement that is transforming publishing.

Our community provides something like the ancient craft system of apprenticeship for authors, but with many masters—all of whom have "been there, done that" and are happy to pay forward what other authors have given to them.

And all of whom are still learning and growing themselves. Hemingway said writers are "apprentices in a craft where no one ever becomes a master". Self-publishing writers are apprentices in *three* crafts where no one ever becomes a master—writing, publishing and creative business.

Perhaps it is most accurate to say that each indie author is both master and apprentice, forever. Our learning is lifelong.

As a self-publisher, you are part of a great flowering of creative expression in the literary arts. Whether you're just starting out, or you're an experienced authorpreneur, ALLi aims to be with you every step of the way.

The experience of its members and advisors is woven into everything we do and everything you'll read in this book. Before we start, I'd like to say a huge thank you to them all.

And I also invite you to join us. You can find out more here: AllianceIndependentAuthors.org.

O rna Ross, London 2020.

A NOTE ABOUT ALLI'S WATCHDOG DESK

C ore to ALLi's mission of ethics and excellence in self-publishing is our **Watchdog Desk**, headed up by John Doppler, author of this book, supported by co-director Philip Lynch, news editor Dan Holloway, and other community watchdogs—two of whom, Victoria Strauss of Writer Beware! and David Gaughran have contributed essays to the introduction.

The watchdog desk helps ALLi members, and the wider indie community, navigate what Victoria Strauss calls the "shark-infested waters" of the self-publishing sector. Our advisors are all independent authors themselves, who dedicate much time and attention to keeping unsuspecting authors out of the hands of poor services.

Also feeding in information and alerts are other community activists like Giacomo (Jim) Giammatteo, ALLi's Enterprise Advisor Joanna Penn, Mick Rooney of The Independent Publishing Magazine, Helen Sedwick, Victoria Strauss of Writer Beware, Mark Williams of The New Publishing Standard, and ALLi's extensive network of authors and approved partners.

But while these high-profile activities attract most attention, ALLi's aim goes beyond highlighting bad actors in the marketplace. Members are also guided towards self-publishing services that have been vetted and approved. These companies and freelancers who are willing to sign up to our **Code of Standards** (see Chapter 17) and guarantee to offer good services, creative solutions, and decent business practices and pricing to authors.

Existing partners range from huge companies like Amazon KDP and Apple iBooks to family businesses and individual freelancers. Many of these are writers themselves (dual membership ensures they benefit from both author and partner privileges) or otherwise embedded in the writing and publishing community.

We are pleased to connect our Author and Partner members and do that in a number of ways. Authors can search for Partners in a **searchable database** in the ALLi Member Zone. We publish an **annual directory** of our Partner Member services that is updated quarterly. Partners can also advertise in the directory and **member magazine**, contribute to our **blog, podcast** and **online conference**, offer **discounts and deals** to authors, **sponsor events** and contribute advice in our **closed forum.**

The Watchdog desk at ALLi also maintains two ratings lists: one of self-publishing services beyond our partner member list; and one of awards and contests. These pages are alphabetical listings of companies under

See: SelfPublishingAdvice.org/ratings for more information to look up a self-publishing service.

See: SelfPublishingAdvice.org/awards to look up an author award or contest.

The information in this book is based on the work of ALLi's hardworking watchdog desk.

PART I

INTRODUCTION

1

HOW TO READ THIS BOOK

Self-publishing is, in many ways, a misnomer. Every good book is a team effort and every good book has been put through the seven processes of publishing that were outlined in Book One of this series: editorial, design, production, distribution, marketing, promotion and rights licensing.

As self-publishing authors we may have some of those skills ourselves but we are going to need to hire others. This book defines the questions we all need to ask about any services we're considering for hire, whether we're publishing our first book, or we have many books in our back list.

The self-publishing services landscape is constantly changing, and as author-publishers, we are all constantly learning and improving, so the services we need change over time.

In making such decisions for your current title, you are doing much more than simply choosing a service; you are adopting a method and a process. Our aim, in this guide, is to outline the options you are most likely to encounter and help you understand which services are optimal for you at this time.

We'll show you which services are doing a good job, and why you might avoid others. Most importantly, in an industry where things are changing so rapidly, we also set the context within which your choices are made.

And provide the criteria by which you can evaluate any self-publishing service yourself.

What should you look out for when trying to compare one service with another in a landscape where they don't all offer the same thing? How do you compare an apple with an orange with a cabbage? We've done our best. Offerings have been categorized, prices examined, royalty structures broken down, terms and conditions trawled, phone calls made, small print scrutinized, and claims checked against the experience of real-life authors who have actually used these services.

At the back of this book, you'll find an index of the most significant service providers, rated against ALLi's Code of Standards. Our assessment process takes into account dozens of criteria, as well as recommendations from our members, warnings from consumer watchdogs, and in-depth research.

How To Read This Book

This book will help you to appraise any service, large or small, *à la carte* or package, and know if it is right for you and whether it represents good value for money.

The best way to approach it is to go to the section which refers to the stage you are at in your author journey. If you're in need of an overview, start at the beginning and read all the way through before beginning your decision-making process. If you are looking for an editor or a marketing service, jump in at chapter 7 or 12. If you haven't made up your mind whether you want to hire a full-service company or individual freelancers, read Part III "Assisted Self-Publishing" first.

All information in this book is up-to-date at time of publication but do bear in mind that the self-publishing sector is always changing. Members questions are answered directly in our member forum and through our Helpdesk.

2

DEFINING OUR TERMS

The publishing industry is now made up of two broad sectors. The first is *self-publishing*, also known as ***author-publishing***, where authors fund and oversee the publication process, using a variety of services to help them produce the book and reach readers but, crucially, retaining all rights.

The second is what used to be called just "publishing" and which we at ALLi now call ***trade-publishing***, where a company other than the author invests in the publishing process in return for a rights license.

These businesses license publishing rights from authors and handle the publication of their books in return for a large percentage, often more than 90% of income (which they must share with wholesalers, distributors and book sellers).

Trade publishing is dominated by corporates with most trade-published books are brought out by one of "The Big Five" corporate publishers: Penguin-Random House; Hachette Book Group (HBG); Harper Collins, Macmillan and Simon & Schuster. Or by an increasingly strong player in the trade publishing market, Amazon Publishing, a branch of Amazon that offer a traditional publishing model. (Self-Publishers work with Amazon KDP, a different part of the Amazon publishing empire).

Authors receive royalties (a percentage of sales revenue) from trade publishers in return for these publishing rights and should receive an advance on those royalty payments on signature of contract, to express the trade publisher's commitment to the author and belief in the book's commercial potential.

But authors now have other pathways to publication and many of them are choosing to publish their books themselves. These independent "indie" authors understand the value of their publishing rights are in addition to self-publishing in ebook, audiobook and print, are selectively licensing some rights e.g. print rights in a certain territory, translation rights, film or TV rights etc. to publishers and other rights buyers.

These indie authors are rapidly changing how the publishing ecosystem operates, but before we go any further we need to define our terms because when we talk about indies and other people in publishing talk about indies, we are not necessarily talking about the same thing.

We also need to define exactly what we mean by self-publishing and how it relates to assisted self-publishing services, vanity publishing, hybrid authors and hybrid publishers, all terms you'll hear once you decide to self-publish a book.

Assisted Self-Publishing

Independent or "Indie" Publishing

Indie authors are not to be confused with indie publishers, small publishing companies which, like the big conglomerates, commission books from authors and publish at the company's expense. They often operate in a particular niche. If very small, they are called micro-publishers. Some authors are now publishing other authors' work in this way.

Hybrid Authors

Hybrid authors is a term used in the past to describe an author who publishes books through both trade and self-publishing platforms. At ALLi, we believe the term "indie author" best describes such a writer as once an author has achieved success in self-publishing they are approached by rights buyers and will selectively license some rights. This is just part of being the creative director of your books and author business.

Hybrid Publishing

Hybrid publishers combine aspects of traditional publishing and self-publishing. They have very varied business models, methods of working with writers, and approaches to marketing and distribution.

Self-Publishing Services

These are services that handle some or all of the processes of publishing, at the author's expense. Services run the gamut from free-lance one-person operations, like designers or editors, to self-publishing services that handle everything for a fee (e.g. BookBaby or Matador), to trade publishers that license rights.

Vanity Services

Vanity presses are a sub-sector of the assisted services sector. The term is a hangover from the days when all author funded publishing was labelled "vanity" by trade publishers. The term has stuck to those services that still trade on authors' dreams of publication to provide sub-standard services.

In ALLi's definition, a vanity service (also known as vanity press or vanity publisher) is one that engages in misleading or deceptive practices, or that

. Vanity services often use trick tactics, bait and switch, and other unethical practices, purely with the intent of extracting maximum money from authors for minimal work on their part.

V anity services are recognised by their intent. Unlike other assisted services, the intention of a vanity press is not to bring books to readers but to extract as much money as possible from the authors.

SELF-PUBLISHING SERVICES

The self-publishing sector therefore offers three separate streams of services for authors:

• **Independent Self-Publishing Services**

For those authors who want to maximise their control and their return on investment.

Companies and freelancers hired by independent, self-publishing "indie" authors who upload their own books directly to self-publishing distributors and operate as the creative director of their book publishing and author business. Services in this sector vary from individual local freelancers to huge, global companies like Amazon KDP and Apple Books.

• A ssisted Self-Publishing Services

For those authors who want more support or who value time more than money.

Companies and sole traders that provide assisted publishing services to authors for a fee. Though assisted, this is still self-publishing, as it is the author who funds the expense of publication. Some of these services bundle the seven processes of publishing into packages. Some offer "hybrid publishing" arrangements that adopt some of the practices of trade publishing, including curation and physical bookstore distribution. Authors shopping in this sector need to exercise caution.

- **Vanity Services**

To be avoided

Controversial sub-stream of the assisted services sector. Vanity services engage in ineffective, sub-standard, misleading or, in the worst cases, outright deceptive practices, with the intention not of bringing books to readers but of extracting as much money as possible from the authors. (Also called "vanity presses" or "vanity publishers").

Also to be avoided are inexperienced or under-performing free-lancers who may mean well but not have the correct information or competencies to do more for your book than you can yourself.

The option to take a more independent route, uploading finished book files directly to one or more of the large online retailers and distributors, directly hiring editors and designers, virtual assistants and marketing services, is the one taken by most ALLi members who make a good income.

This means making choices that maximize your creative and commercial advantage, drawing together online tools and collabora-tors to supplement your own competencies and self-taught skills, and getting stuck into hands-on book preparation and production: learning by doing.

First time out, it takes the author on a steep learning curve, which is why some people like to break themselves in gently by starting with the support of a full-service package.

Yes, the independent option is most likely to give a commercial return on the author's investment of time and money but juggling multiple service providers can create additional overhead and headaches in the form of research, billing, and coordination.

Time-strapped authors may instead choose to purchase a comprehensive, full-service publishing package from a single vendor for the convenience, or a smaller bundle of related services.These packages tend to have a higher price tag, and the author usually pays a premium for the convenience of one-stop shopping and more personalised service.

Contrary to what you might hear from some authors, not all

assisted services charging higher-end fees are a waste of money, or dishonest, or vanity services by definition. As in any other

It's not a question of price, but of value for money. What are you paying for? Does it have real tangible value in terms of helping you to produce a great book or reach more readers?

Authors must understand the value being offered and the values of the service company making the offer. In general, ALLi recommends purchasing services on an *à la carte* basis rather than as a package of bundled services. When services are separate, it's easier to assess the quality, value, and performance of each. Breaking out services individually also eliminates the common problem of package bloat, in which low-value, high-markup services are used to pad the perceived value (and cost) of a package. (See Chapter 16).

Check terms and conditions as some service contracts may limit your opportunities and control. Control of your rights, control of your metadata, control of your positioning, marketing and promotion are rights that are not to be given up lightly, to either a trade-publisher or a self-publishing service.

Every author should at least consider the independent option of keeping as much control as possible, hiring freelance assistance for editorial and design, and uploading books directly to self-publishing platforms like Amazon and Apple. But if you can afford it, and it makes sense in your circumstances, having a reputable company hold your hand through the process can be comforting and make things easier to negotiate, especially first time out.

Be aware that it is in the package end of the self-publishing market that we find most of the rogue providers. Check ALLi's Directory of Services to find our approved Partner Members.

If you've heard of a service and are unsure whether it is legitimate, you can check our Service Ratings page here.

3
<hr>

PUBLISHERS DON'T ASK FOR PAYMENT

This has long been the position of savvy authors. A trade-publisher pays you. A self-publishing service is paid by you. In recent times, there have been huge changes in the self-publishing sector and so it is not always so clearcut now. Varied business models, methods of working with writers, and approaches to marketing and distribution are emerging, including companies attempting to straddle the line between both models, offering a traditional publishing framework, but charging the author to offset the cost of production.

Sometimes referred to as subsidy publishing or joint publishing, hybrid publisher is the term most widely used to describe this crossbreed of publisher and self-publishing service.

Hybrid presses are an usual exception to the rule that publishers don't ask for payment. Authors must be wary of questionable services that use this exception to justify exploitative charges.

And of vanity presses that use this more acceptable term to cover up exploitative practices.

There are legitimate hybrid publishers but, as ALLi Advisor Jane Friedman puts it, "the term has become popular among companies that wish to put a new, "innovative" face on a very common, age-old activity: charging writers to publish" while not doing the most challenging parts of the publishing process: marketing and promotion and rights licensing.

Adding to the complexity is the confusion between hybrid publishers and so-called "hybrid authors". These are *not*, as you might think, authors who work with hybrid publishing companies. Instead, that term is used by some to describe authors who both traditionally publish and self-publish. (Though at ALLi we think the term indie author adequately covers this).

And to add even more murk to the mix, some trade publishers, including Penguin Random House and Simon & Schuster, have aligned with the worst self-publishing companies.

No wonder authors are confused.

In this section we look at the various kinds of assisted self-publishing services, the kind you should avoid, and those that may be worth your money, depending on your circumstances.

4

THE INDEPENDENT AUTHOR

BY ALLI DIRECTOR ORNA ROSS

O nce upon a time, when I started out as a writer, publishing ran on a scarcity model. It was difficult for an author to find a publisher and even to find writing or publishing advice. Now, we have an abundance model: a plethora of publishing choices, and advice on every side. The problem for an author or aspiring author today is not a tight, closed system but a confusing cornucopia of choice.

The first-time self-publisher is often overcome with questions. How do I make a book? How do I get it to readers? What services and supports do I need? How much will it cost me? How much can I make?

Starting out, many writers type "self-publishing" into a Google search and instantly find themselves drowning in jargon and entries highjacked by vanity services, winding up completely confused. The answers to their questions are there, but rarely on the first page and framed in a hundred different ways by a thousand different people.

If our tyro author keeps going, soon an additional suite of questions emerge. How much should an editor cost? How do I protect my copyright? What is an ISBN? Do I need one? Is it worth paying for promotion? Where do I find good services that won't rip me off?

Writers must find answers in an environment where some services are run by people who are knowledgeable, dedicated, helpful, and fair while others are clueless, greedy, callous, and manipulative; where the same service can cost $500 or $15,000 depending on where you shop; and where many of the worst services dominate the information stream, including Facebook and Google Ads and search, trapping unwary writers into thinking they are publishers, not self-publishing services.

No wonder even experienced authors feel overwhelmed by this unregulated market that is highly creative, innovative, and exciting, yes, but also idiosyncratic, illogical, and incoherent.

PUBLISHING TODAY

In that same "once upon a time" before the internet unlocked literary doors, there was a simple divide in place. On the one hand, you had trade publishers and they paid you. On the other, you had vanity publishers, and you paid them.

If you worked with the former, you were entitled to call yourself "published" and revel in the fact that somebody besides your mother thought you'd something worth saying for yourself.

If you were the one reaching for your wallet, you were thought to be vain and deluded, and deserving of every thing you were being dealt from the assorted literary fraudsters chasing your dream.

Almost. Even back then, there were determined and self-motivated authors who used self-publishing to break through. Writers like Jill Patton Walsh, whose book *Knowledge of Angels* was shortlisted for the Booker Prize. Writers like Wayne Dyer, who put his self-published books on the back of his car and went from town to town across America doing promotional talks, until they became bestsellers and were picked up by a trade publisher.

The vanity accusation was a good way of keeping authors feeling insecure, the implication being that if their book couldn't find a publisher, it was because it wasn't good enough. That this assumption was deeply wrong has been revealed by the new self-publishing technologies.

Manuscripts from aspiring writers that would once have been relegated to what trade-publishers charmingly call "the slush pile" are now finding engaged readers and avid fans.

In the past, paying for publication was largely a vain effort because self-publishing rarely worked. The distribution of books was a tightly controlled, print-only supply chain and it was almost impossible for a writer with a garage full of books to break in, no matter how good the book might be.

These days we need to ask more specific questions about the "vanity" label. Ego is something all authors trade in, inherent in the very desire to have other people read your opinions, stories or ideas, but the vanity question is one that each author must answer for themselves.

While we can all see the vanity in paying a large sum of money to a self-publishing services that is experienced in flattery (they love your book) and deceptive practices (they would love to "publish" it), is it really vanity to take a risk on your own skills and hard work, with your time and money? To dream and work for the day when you will make a good living as an author?

Or is it vanity to value the validation of an exclusive deal with a trade publisher over the work of developing your own publishing skills and reaching your readers yourself?

Today, the term "vanity publisher" is usually used to describe inadequate self-publishing services that deliberately exploit authors' publishing ambitions. ALLi's definition of a vanity press is one that engages in misleading or deceptive practices with the intention not of bringing books to readers but of extracting as much money as possible from the authors. See Chapter 15 for more on this.

AUTHOR PUBLISHING TODAY

There are three kinds of author-publishers, distinguished by their reasons for publishing their own work and their attitude to readers and author business. At ALLi, we give them different names, so we know who we are talking about, and how to best serve them.

Self-publishing Authors

The self-publisher is primarily interested in writing, and in the content and look of the book. They have little interest in marketing, promotion, rights sales or author-business. They "publish" their work in the sense of producing it and making it publicly available but not in the sense of acting like a commercial publisher.

For these writers, publication is primarily self-expression. They are less interested in reaching readers than in expressing something and putting it out there. Often, they are publishing a book for family, friends or their own community.They may, or may not, produce well-crafted writing and may or may not produce well-crafted books. One way or the other, they generally get a great deal out of the publishing experience.

Indie Authors

These authors want to write, produce and sell their own books and establish a successful author business. Some arrive at this stage from having produced one book and now wanting to take it further: find readers, earn money, set up in author business. Others know before they've formatted a word that this is their ambition.

Indie authors are the core of ALLi's membership, "indie", not because it allows writers to borrow some secondhand cool from the worlds of film and music but because an independent growth mindset is core to what we do: our most defining feature, our most essential tool.

At ALLi, we spot when a self-publisher goes indie. The defining difference is that they think beyond the first book. They start setting and meeting creative goals and intentions. Soon they are finishing more books and reaching more readers, learning from their mistakes, experiments and explorations, and taking the lessons into the next book.

It takes the writer on the creative ride of their life and most need a good deal of help and support at the start to understand what it is to be an indie author, and meet the new ideas and challenges. If they come to self-publishing thinking it's second-best to trade-publishing, they can go through a tough time at first, and are more likely to fall away, defeated not so much by the work needed, as the attitude they've brought to the work.

Those who stay the course begin to engage with, not resist, the work inherent in good publishing: working with suitable beta readers and editors; understanding where their books fit in the wider publishing ecosystem; learning what genres and format and categories fit their projects; discovering what they have to say; finding their voice.

Authorpreneurs

Authorpreneurs are succeeding in author business. They have adopted an independent, creative growth mindset and embrace the idea that marketing and business, as well as writing, can be creative. They have mastered three different sets of skills: writing good books, publishing them well, and running an author business, a significant creative and commercial achievement.

And they are consciously applying entrepreneurial skills and mindset and digital tools to making a sustainable and ongoing living as an author.

They know how to promote, market, sell and profit from their writing, not as a once-off, but through the dedicated application of one of their chosen business model.

Authorpreneur is a made-up word (author + entrepreneur), a new word for a new kind of job. Some dislike it, thinking it faddy or forced, but it is gaining traction in the self-publishing sector because there is no other word that so well describes this kind of author.

Today digital tools and tech are seeing entrepreneurial authors emerging in far greater number than ever before. ALLi has a specific membership category for authorpreneurs.

Becoming an Indie Author

For both the serial indie author and the one-book self-publisher, "self" publishing is a misnomer. It implies that we do it all alone, when actually every good book is a team effort. "Independent," too is a relative term. Indie authors are relatively independent, compared to trade-published authors, because we retain our publishing rights and control over our book production, distribution and marketing.

But we rely on our editors and designers, self-publishing platforms and social media, not to mention our readers.

Some of our members are fiercely autonomous, as DIY as it's possible to be, actively advocating the self-publishing route for all and envisaging the imminent end of trade-publishing. While these members of the community are vocal, the majority of authors are happy to collaborate with a publishing service where that seems advantageous, or for particular projects, whether that's a paid self-publishing service, or a trade-publisher offering an advance.

What, then, marks out an "indie" author? For ALLi, you satisfy the following conditions:

• You have self-published at least one book.

• You see yourself as the creative director of your books, from conception to completion through marketing, promotion, and beyond.

• You also see yourself as the creative director of your author-business. In any partnership you negotiate, whether with a self-publishing service, a trade-publisher or a literary agent, you expect your status as rights holder and creative director to be acknowledged in payment, terms and conditions.

• You are proud of your indie status and carry that self-respect into your ventures, negotiations and collaborations, for your own benefit and the benefit of the reading and writing community.

THE VALUE OF ASSISTANCE

Thanks to digital tools, putting a book out is getting easier all the time. Publishing well, however, is more than book production, it is the seven processes outlined in Book 1: *Creative Self-Publishing: Making and Selling Your Book Your way*

1. Editorial
2. Design
3. Production
4. Distribution
5. Marketing
6. Promotion
7. Rights licensing

Presenting and positioning a book in a way that makes it accessible and attractive to readers, and reaching as many of those readers as possible, is as hard for the author as it is for anyone else. And is as hard today as it ever was.

Before you hire your next service, ask yourself why you want this particular form of assistance.

Maybe you want a service that will take away the tasks you don't want to do, leaving you free to write? That's an understandable desire, but before you make the decision, ensure that's what you'll be getting. Know not just what you're paying your service to do (you'll find help with that below) but also other options and alternative routes.

Too often, authors choose self-publishing packages because they are frightened by the technology. The shift in power toward the author that self-publishing promises makes many people uncomfortable, including many writers.

And with the control and freedom delivered by self-publishing comes responsibility, and that can be daunting. Often, it is in trying to avoid this responsibility that writers hire second-rate or problematic services. The danger is that the fear factor could see us selling ourselves short.

Other dangers are being seduced by slick advertising, fear of learning or technology, or not knowing your options.

Choosing a service is an important decision—with expensive consequences if you get it wrong. The more you want the service to do for you, the more you need to stop and consider. As with any serious investment, shop around before you buy.

- Ask the right questions, know the depth and quality of service you are getting, and educate yourself on the alternative options.
- Understand what they are charging you for, and how much money they are taking and, crucially, what they are asking for in terms of rights.
- Take note of the service's intent. Are they in the business of publishing good books and reaching as many readers as possible? Look at other books they have produced to help you decide.

You *can* work your way through the maze of services and find the services that are right for you, whether that is a one-off freelance assistance or a full publishing package.

If you have further questions don't hesitate to contact us at AllianceIndependentAuthors.org.

5

WRITER BEWARE

BY VICTORIA STRAUSS

I f you've completed a book and want to publish it, you might think it makes sense to turn to Google. You are not alone. "How to publish a book" is a popular internet search phrase.

This is not a great idea.

While such searches turn up some good resources, a lot of what you'll see on the first couple of pages (which is as far as most people look), is useless or worse. The internet is an invaluable resource. But it's also a tsunami of misinformation and a shark pit of scammers and opportunists.

Yes, there are sharks out there in the literary waters. The writer who wants to publish or self-publish a book needs to know that literary deceptions abound, from fee-charging literary agents to dishonest editors to deceptive vanity publishers to fake contests.

"Publishers" offering a contract that requires you to pay for publication are not publishers. Such companies are variously known as vanity, subsidy, joint-venture, co-op, or partner publishers.

Often, you're told that what you're paying is only a portion of the cost, with the publisher kicking in the rest or providing additional services of substantial value. In reality, most pay-to-publish ventures charge inflated prices that not only cover the whole cost of production, but generate fat profits for the service.

Most insidious are the websites that purport to match you with appropriate publishers in exchange for information about yourself and your book. The true purpose of these sites isn't to provide helpful guidance to writers, but to generate leads for author services companies and vanity publishers, which either pay for listings or buy the information gathered through the forms writers fill out.

Another trap: listings for faux consumer guides where overpriced author services companies pay for advertising, and misleading "Top 10" lists which are really just a bunch of pay-per-click affiliate links. (There's a reason why so many of these sites list the same companies.)

Be skeptical in general of any resource that claims to list the Top Anything--at best, this will be subjective and incomplete--or that presents itself as a consumer resource (unless you can verify that it is, in fact, a consumer resource).

That's why they want your phone number and mailing address, and why many of them ask how much you're willing to pay for publication. If you go through the process of filling out the forms, you'll either be promised direct contact from "interested publishers" (read: relentless phone solicitations from author services companies), or given a list of "personalized" recommendations--all of which are pay-to-play.

Many of these sites neglect to say who sponsors them, and have anonymized domain registrations. Some can be traced back to lead generation or affiliate marketing companies, but figuring out their provenance can be difficult.

Unless they're owned by the granddaddy of author services companies, Author Solutions.

Author Solutions is by far the largest sponsor of fake publisher matching sites, all designed to steer writers into the clutches of AS's many "imprints". AS does identify itself in tiny print at the bottom of the sites, or in the sites' privacy policies. But these mild disclosures can easily be missed by eager writers, who in any case may not be familiar with AS's reputation for high prices, aggressive solicitation, poor customer service, and junk marketing. (And seriously, who reads privacy policies?)

Writer Beware Organization

Writer Beware was founded in 1998 by myself and fellow author and Science Fiction and Fantasy Writers of America (SFWA) member Ann Crispin (**A.C. Crispin**), who has since sadly passed away. Like the ALLi Watchdog desk, Writer Beware!'s mission has always been to track, expose, and raise awareness of scams and other questionable activities in and around the publishing industry

Around the time I first went online, in the mid 1990's, several major scams were just beginning to implode, in part through writers' discussion of their experiences on the Internet. I was at first fascinated, and then horrified, by this fraudulent shadow-industry. Here was a whole slimy publishing underworld that I'd had no idea existed.

Writer Beware is entirely staffed by volunteers. We're sponsored by the **Science Fiction and Fantasy Writers of America**, with additional support from the **Mystery Writers of America**. Although SFWA and MWA are US-based organizations of professional genre fiction authors, Writer Beware's efforts aren't limited by genre, country, or publication history.

ALLi and Writer Beware! have tracked the amazing growth of self-publishing schemes and scams over the past few years. Self-publishers face a wide array of dangers, from "editing services" that do little more than run manuscripts through spelling and grammar checks, to overpriced designers and artists and formatting services, to bogus publicists who charge a premium for junk-mail "marketing," to predatory self-publishing services that advertise themselves misleadingly and engage in relentless upselling.

Lack of competence is also a big problem. There are skilled providers for every step of the self-publishing process, but there are also many people offering services—often for a lot of money—that they aren't qualified to deliver. These people may not be scammers; in fact, they may have the best of intentions. But goodwill is not a substitute for experience. For most writers, the difference between a scammer and an amateur is negligible: either way, they wind up with a smaller bank account and an inferior product.

The good news is that you can protect yourself, with a little information and a healthy dose of caution.

WHEN YOU SHOULD BE CAUTIOUS

If a Literary agent Requires an Upfront fee.

Reputable literary agents derive their income from commissions on the sale of literary properties, and not from upfront fees.

Asking for money upfront violates the basic premise of the author-agent relationship: a shared financial interest in the sale of the author's manuscript. An agent who profits only when the author does is highly motivated not just to place a manuscript with a paying publisher, but to obtain the best possible deal. An agent who makes money right off the bat has already made a profit, diminishing the incentive to submit to legitimate publishers.

There are three kinds of upfront fee you may encounter. The first is **the reading fee**: a request for money just to read your manuscript. It's not hard to imagine how this practice can be abused, which is why most professional agents' associations prohibit it for their members. No reputable agent charges reading fees–in fact, they're so discredited that very few fraudulent agents charge them either.

The second kind of upfront fee is **the evaluation fee**. Agents who charge evaluation fees promise not just to read your manuscript, but to provide a critique. But evaluation fees are as easy to abuse as reading fees–which is why they too are proscribed by most agents' associations.

The third (and by far the most common) kind of upfront fee is **the "marketing" or "submission" or "administrative" or "handling" or** "**retainer**" **fee**–supposedly, a share of the expense of marketing a manuscript.

Confusion arises here, because most reputable agents do expect clients to bear some of the cost of submission. However, a reputable agents will pass on only *unusual* expenses (expenses incurred on the client's behalf over and above the ordinary cost of doing business, such as photocopying, postage, long-distance calls, Fed Ex, etc.–with so much business done electronically these days, these expenses are usually minimal), and to either accrue them and deduct them from the author's advance, or bill them after they're incurred.

Questionable agents, by contrast, want expense money right away–usually as a lump sum on contract signing, but sometimes as a monthly or quarterly allowance, or a per-submission fee. They may also expect clients to pay not just for the unusual expenses described above, but for every file folder, envelope, and paper clip, or for unnec-essary extras–photos, business cards, marketing plans, fancy bindings.

Some agents who charge marketing fees are con artists. Most, however, are simply inept, and can't keep their businesses afloat without putting their hands in their clients' pockets. Either way, a marketing fee, like a reading or evaluation fee, is a warning sign–if not of outright dishonesty, then of an unsuccessful business.

If a "Publisher" offers a Contract that Requires you to Pay for Publication.

There are vanity publishers that will deliver what they promise, but others are dishonest–concealing their fees, advertising services they don't provide, lying about producing print runs (you may have paid for 2,500 books, but only the 100 copies you were given to distribute to friends and reviewers were ever printed), failing to pay royalties owed...the list goes on. Plus, because vanity publishers will publish pretty much anyone who will pay, books from such publishers have a bad rap with readers, booksellers, and reviewers.

Vanity publishers often pitch themselves to new writers by saying that the risk involved in publishing an unknown makes cost-sharing necessary, or that making an "investment" in your book proves you're serious about a writing career. Don't believe it.

If an Agent or Publisher asks you to Pay for Adjunct Services.

One of the objects of getting published is for you to earn money. If instead you find yourself reaching for your wallet, something isn't right.

If you're referred to an outside service–such as a publicist or independent editor–it's possible that a kickback arrangement is involved. The agent or publisher may have been promised a finder's fee for successful referrals, or a percentage of whatever you wind up paying for the service. Some vanity publishers also engage in kickback schemes, offering agents a bonus for each client they persuade to accept a pay-to-publish contract.

Alternatively, the agency or publisher may own the service (possibly under a different name, so you won't spot the connection). A publisher might steer writers to its own critique or evaluation service. A literary agency might run a separate editing branch, and require writers to obtain a critique as a condition of representation. Or it might own a vanity publisher, into which clients are funneled once they've racked up enough rejections to become desperate. All of these are serious conflicts of interest: if the recommendation to use a service can make money for the recommender, how can a writer trust that his or her best interest is being served?

There are times when a reputable agent may suggest that a writer hire an independent editor–for instance, for a salable project that needs developmental work that the author, in the agent's judgment, can't provide. Such recommendations can be perfectly legitimate–though you should do some careful thinking before deciding to go this often very expensive route. But questionable editing schemes are common, and receiving an editing referral should always make you wary.

If You're Asked to buy Something as a Condition of Publication

An increasing number of vanity publishers are trying to dodge the vanity label by shifting their charges to some aspect of publication other than printing and binding. Instead of asking you to pay to print your book, they ask you to buy goods or services.

You may be asked to purchase editing, or to fund a publicity campaign, or to hire the company's own artistic or design staff. You may have to agree to buy a large number of your own books, or to become a salesperson and sell your books prior to publication. You may be asked to buy or sell ads for your book, or to pay to attend the publisher's expensive conferences, or to purchase the publisher's other books. The bottom line in all these situations is the same: you are paying to see your work in print.

There are also many poetry and short story anthologies that pressure writers to buy the anthology in which they're included. Vanity anthology companies often solicit business via a fake contest, offering publication to everyone who submits. Vanity anthologizers may also bombard writers with solicitations to buy other things–their poem mounted on a plaque, their story made into an audiotape, membership in an authors' registry maintained by the company, attendance at a writers' conference hosted by the company. Writer Beware has heard from writers who've wound up spending thousands of dollars this way.

Because vanity anthologies employ no editorial screening and offer publication to anyone who enters their "contests", they aren't considered a genuine literary market. As with a vanity-published book, inclusion in one of these anthologies will not count as a professional writing credit.

If You're Solicited

Reputable agents and publishers will sometimes reach out to writers whose blogs they've read, or whose articles or stories they've seen.

However, if you're solicited out of the blue, it's far more likely that the person or company wants your money.

Some questionable agents and publishers buy subscription lists from writers' magazines. Others solicit writers who register their copyrights. Still others cruise websites, blogs, and writers' forums.

On a related note: reputable agents and publishers often maintain websites, but they rarely advertise. Beware of the literary agent or publisher ads you find the backs of writers' magazines, or see online. And remember, Google is not always your friend. Typing "literary agent" or "book publisher" into a search engine is guaranteed to turn up scammers.

If Requests for Information are Refused.

It's your right to ask an agent or publisher or independent editor about their track record, contract terms, commissions, marketing, distribution, and so on. If they're reputable, they should be glad to answer. Questionable agents and publishers and editors, on the other hand, are often very reluctant to provide information–for good reason.

Be especially wary of an agent who tells you that his/her sales list is confidential. Reputable agents won't always be willing to reveal their entire client list, but they shouldn't have a problem telling you about recent sales (if they have a website or other online listing, the information should be available there). An agent who won't provide this information may be trying to conceal a poor track record.

If there's a Double Standard or a Special Deal

An agent may tell you that she usually charges a reading fee, but because your query is so terrific she'll read your manuscript for free. Or a publisher may claim that while it usually offers advances, for new authors there's a special "joint venture" deal. Or an independent editor may say that he usually charges $5.00 per page, but if you send in your manuscript right away he'll give you a 20% discount.

Don't be fooled. You aren't receiving special treatment, just a calculated marketing pitch. The agent hopes that if you think you're getting a freebie on the reading, you'll be more willing to pay the marketing fee she plans to ask for later on. The publisher wants you to believe it's a "real" publisher, when in fact expensive vanity contracts are probably the only kind it offers. The editor thinks that if he can convince you that you're getting a bargain, you'll be more likely to buy his services.

Choosing A Self-Publishing Service

There are scores of self-publishing services offering a range of prices —from free to five figures—and features. Only by comparing one with another and getting to know what's possible can you be sure to find the best match for your needs and goals.

Be educated. A good knowledge base is your best defense against schemes and scams. Take the time to learn about self-publishing before jumping into it. As well as this book, see also ALLi's Self-Publishing Advice Centre (selfpublishingadvice.org) and Writer Beware! (accrispin.blogspot.com).

Be social. Hang out with other self-publishers—you'll learn a lot from both their successes and their mistakes. ALLi's member forum is invaluable. See also the Kindle boards and Absolute Write Water Cooler.

Be smart. For any person or service you're thinking of hiring, check references, credentials, and reputations.

Don't take anything at face value. You can contact ALLi's Watchdog Desk or Writer Beware and ask. If we've received any reports of problems with a particular service, we'll let you know.

Successful self-publishing is hard work. Be prepared to get out of it what you put into it. Good luck!

6

THE VALUE OF CONTROL
BY DAVID GAUGHRAN

The key advantage of self-publishing is control. If you self-publish, you get to pick yourself instead of waiting (maybe forever) to be picked. You get to choose an appropriate cover for your book, not one foisted on you by a publisher anxious to move onto the next batch of titles. And you get to set a price that will encourage readers to take a chance on an unknown author, instead of being overpriced and ignored. Control is also important in other fundamental ways that won't be obvious until you start self-publishing and trying to reach readers.

Marketing

It's obvious from talking to prospective self-publishers that marketing is the task that causes the most stress and trepidation. Of course, scammy operators know this. They prey on these fears by offering a series of magic bullets at exorbitant prices. And they don't work.

At all!

I can prove this. Take the vanity press of your choice. Search for the publisher name on Amazon. Check the ranking of the book that comes up first (that should be the one selling best). See how poorly it's doing? Read the stories of successful self-publishers. Notice how none of them have used a vanity press. Notice how none of them recommend the kind of marketing being sold by the vanity presses (such as spamming millions of people who don't care about your book or buying YouTube advertising packages). That should tell you something.

At this stage, I've tried almost everything in terms of marketing and can draw clear lines between what's effective and what isn't when it comes to promoting books. And I think I can put your mind at ease. Out of all the marketing tools at your disposal, the ones that tend to take up too much time, cost a lot of money, or make you feel uncomfortable tend to be the least effective.

So what is effective? In proof of the ultimate serendipity of the universe, the tools that actually shift books in meaningful numbers won't cost too much, eat into your writing time, or make you feel like a slimy huckster.

The stuff that is actually proven to work includes things like running a limited-time $0.99 sale, especially in conjunction with a reasonably priced ad on a reputable reader site. Other powerful promotional tools don't even cost anything, such as building a mailing list of readers that are genuinely interested in your work. Or making the first book in your series cheap or free. Or getting together with a group of authors in the same genre to cross-promote your books.

You can find plenty of information online about these marketing techniques, but the important thing to note for now is that you will not be able to use them if you go with a vanity press or other self-publishing service that doesn't give you control of your book's product page at the various retailers.

In the rest of this book, you will have been given innumerable reasons to avoid vanity presses like AuthorHouse, Xlibris, iUniverse, Trafford, Balboa Press, Archway, WestBow, and Abbot Press. I want to give you a few more reasons. When you sign up with a self-publishing "service" like this, you lose control in the following ways.

Incorrect Categories

You won't be able to directly control which category your book appears in on the various retailers. This is crucial for both discoverability and visibility. All the retailers have a huge variety of virtual shelves your book can appear on, and these can be quite granular. In a physical bookstore, books tend to be divided up into quite general categories like self-help, romance, science fiction, and thrillers. Online retailers like Amazon have much more specific categories like post-apocalyptic science fiction or political thrillers. And they give you the ability to place each book on several such virtual shelves.

Getting on the right virtual shelf is incredibly important. You need your book to appear to readers who are interested in it. There is zero value in your epic space opera series appearing to readers searching for inspirational Christian romance. And the only way to ensure your book will appear on the right shelf on Amazon is by uploading directly to Kindle Direct Publishing (KDP). If you use an intermediary service, there is a strong likelihood that you won't get in the most appropriate granular subcategory for your book, and a reasonable chance you will get put in either a useless general category like fiction or on the wrong shelf altogether.

Changing Price

Many vanity presses don't let you change your book's price at all, and others charge a fee for any such price changes. Even when you can change price, it can take days or weeks to take effect. But when you are running a limited-time sale you need to be able to change your price within hours, not days. The only way to control price in this manner is to upload directly to Amazon's KDP.

Measuring Success

All the major ebook retailers (Amazon, Barnes & Noble, Apple, and Kobo) provide up-to-date sales figures in your account interface. This is crucial for measuring the effectiveness of any marketing. These near-live sales figures allow you to know what works and what doesn't, and the results can often be counterintuitive. For example, I learned that being interviewed in the *Sunday Times* shifts fewer books than taking out a $20 ad with a small reader site. It's nice to appear in a newspaper, of course, but knowing the precise value of that exposure shows me what kind of attention I should actively pursue.

If you use a vanity press or self-publishing service to publish your books, you won't have up-to-date sales figures at all. You will be flying blind, unable to measure the effectiveness of your marketing efforts. Without this data, you won't be able to know what was a waste of time and money, and what's worth trying again.

Keeping Control

There's a simple way to keep control of all this stuff and give your book the best possible chance of success, and the best thing about it is it won't cost you a penny. Uploading to Amazon is free, until the point that you make a sale. Uploading to Kobo is free. And instead of paying a fee or percentage to access those marketplaces, you will keep all your royalties.

Getting into Apple necessitates owning a Mac (and the process can be daunting) and there are many other retailers, but you can have access to them by using a reputable distributor like Smashwords or Draft2Digital. These services don't charge upfront fees and only take a small percentage of your royalties at the point of sale.

Don't fall for the vanity press propaganda. It's not "easier" to pay a lump sum and have someone take care of all this for you; it will end up causing far more heartache in the end when they publish your book in a substandard way. Worst of all, you won't be able to use the proven marketing techniques of successful self-publishers.

Your book deserves better. You deserve better. Keep control.

PART II

THE SEVEN PROCESSES OF PUBLISHING

7

WRITING SERVICES

J ust as there are seven stages to publishing, the first stage, writing, can be divided into seven stages.

The first five stages of the writing process occur before you get into self-editing. After that, having done as much editing as you can yourself, you bring in others but for those first five stages of the process, you must do most of the work yourself.

1. **Intention:** Deciding what you are going to write about and the form: book, article, poem, short story.
2. **Incubation:** Germinating the idea, making notes.
3. **Investigation:** Researching the idea in sources, memory and imagination, making more notes.
4. **Composition:** Writing the first draft.
5. **Amplification:** Deepening your ideas and improving the overall shape of your manuscript.
6. **Clarification:** editing and self-editing (more on this in the next chapter, editorial services).
7. **Completion:** incorporating notes from beta readers and final preparations of the typescript for your editor .

You can feel quite alone through some of these stages and there are some writing services that aim to support you in getting the book through to completion.

These service providers may keep you writing, assess your work and give feedback, and offer other tools that help you find your way through to editing stage (covered in the next section).

Coaching and Mentoring

For novice authors and experienced authors alike, one-on-one time with a writing coach can be a helpful tool in the early stages of writing. It's important to find the right mentor who understands your project and your needs, and has a compatible work style and ethic.

Depending on what you need, a mentor can act as a sounding board to help work through plot and characterization issues; help find the best structure, style, and tone; or even give you writing assignments to get your brain working though writer's block. It's a versatile tool because it's a creative relationship that takes on the needs of each individual project.

There are several considerations you'll want to examine when evaluating a writing coach, but foremost is experience. There is a tendency among some authors to consider themselves experts upon attaining some small measure of success.

The Dunning-Kruger effect comes into sharp focus here. These individuals may not have the experience to recognize their shortcomings, and so they may misjudge their knowledge and skill. They may assume that all authors' processes are similar to their own, and may then find themselves at a loss when your circumstances don't align with theirs.

Investigate your prospective coach's credentials and history to ensure they have the expertise to guide authors in a wide variety of situations.

Genre is another important consideration. While there is considerable overlap in the challenges authors of various genres face, the differences between them can be extreme. Confirm that your prospective coach has experience in your specific genre.

Finally, you'll want to consider whether the coach or mentor's personality is compatible with yours. Personality is a key factor in a successful coaching relationship. Some personality traits simply don't work well together, and you may not discover this friction until you've had an opportunity to work with the prospective mentor.

A good writing coach will allow for an introductory period in which you'll both learn whether your styles are compatible. Look for coaches who offer a trial period or a suitable refund policy should you decide that the relationship isn't going to work.

Manuscript Appraisal

Manuscript appraisal is a good tool to use when you're not sure if you've gone in the right direction. Having someone look at your manuscript objectively offers a writer not only an idea of how readers will receive the book but also concrete information about stylistic choices, plot, and characterization.

The major difference between an appraisal and an actual edit is that the end product of an appraisal is a report that details the general workings of the manuscript. The assessor leaves the author to consider the feedback and make any applicable changes. The report discusses structure, plot development, story pacing, and characterization for fiction; structure, pacing, and samples and examples for nonfiction. And for both, these reports discuss reader engagement, tone, and overall strengths and weaknesses.

Experience is the key factor when evaluating a manuscript appraiser. You are looking for a professional who can offer more in-depth feedback than a critique group of peers. Ask about their credentials. Ask how they approach the process. Ask how they will help make your manuscript the best it can be.

When you've found a manuscript appraiser with a positive track record, it's time to consider value. It's difficult to quantify how much value services like editing and appraisal will bring to your book, but keep the long view in mind. Think about how many copies of your book you would need to sell to offset the cost. Over the lifetime of your book, is it a reasonable figure?

Ghostwriting

Ghostwriting happens when, for whatever reason, a client is unable to write their project. A ghostwriter will step in and complete the writing, but it's still a creative collaboration. The client and ghostwriter work together on structure, voice, plot, etc., but the ghostwriter, although their name may never appear on the cover, is the sole content creator.

Ghostwriting services are frequently offered by disreputable vanity presses, especially those who prey on business leaders looking to promote themselves. Authors who employ ghostwriters must take great care to ensure that they're receiving the quality, depth, and value they expect.

8

EDITORIAL SERVICES

Every writer needs at least one editor. We do not see our own work clearly, and a fresh set of eyes is essential to catch mistakes and oversights in our manuscripts, no matter how perfect we think they are. The best writers in the world are edited into publication; it is a mistake for indie authors to believe we can DIY this. Usually, it's what we don't know we don't know that lets our books down.

Editing ourselves to some degree is, of course, necessary, and the sixth stage of the writing process. But going over and over our manuscript in the effort to avoid hiring an editor is a waste of valuable writing time (and can actually be a sophisticated form of creative resistance, stopping us from moving briskly through the publication of the current book and onto the next).

Investing time in finding the right editor and investing money in the proper service are vital. A good editor is invaluable. In the early stages, in addition to adding ideas, asking open questions, and suggesting solutions, they will appreciate and reinforce your creative intentions.

Worthwhile editing services will add to the professional look and quality of your book, bring major problems to your attention, and help you with problem areas you have identified. But not all editing is the same, and as you progress through the process of writing, you'll need different levels and types of editing.

It's important to understand what type of editing you need and to base price and time expectations accordingly. For example, content editing can be more time-consuming than a proofread, and prices will be reflective of that.

Editing and Self-Editing

Editing is a stage in both the writing process and the publishing process. The final two stages of the writing process are

6. Clarification

7. Completion.

It's important not to confuse the clarification stage of the writing process, during which you do lots of self-editing, with the editing that is done after the completion stage by other readers and professionals: beta readers, copy-editors, line editors, and proof-readers.

Self-editing is what *you* do, as you write the book and as you work with writing services to improve it. Then, when you have done all you can do, when you can't see another improvement that can be made, you bring in your editors.

This editing work is what separates professional writers from amateurs and both kinds—self-editing and professional editing—are essential. One is not a substitute for the other.

Developmental/Content Editing

As you shape up your first draft and need a first reader, or if you are in need of guidance for a widespread problem around pacing, plotting, or character development in later drafts, then content editing is what you're looking for. (This can also be called book doctoring, manuscript appraisal, structural editing, substantive editing, and many other names, as these terms are used loosely and in divergent ways. Check with the service provider to verify exactly what you're getting.)

Whatever it's called, content editing is a down-and-deep look at the manuscript that is likely to require major rewrites. This level may identify outstanding grammar and punctuation errors, but is more focused on the big picture.

At the point of needing this editing service, you are still several passes away from being ready to publish.

Copyediting/Line Editing

Once you are satisfied that you have a solid manuscript and are finished making major changes, you can move on to copyediting/line editing. At this stage, editors will be doing a thorough scrub of the manuscript, looking for things like:

- consistency, grammatical errors, style
- factual errors (especially important in nonfiction books)
- fluidity of language
- aesthetics such as the overuse of certain words, phrases, hyphens, or fragmented sentences
- linguistic efficiency.

This phase of editing leaves you with a clean manuscript ready for design and layout of the final output.

Proofreading

The final step in any professionally produced manuscript is proofreading. When your manuscript has gone through its final edits, design, and layout, a proofread will find any final errors that have slipped through the cracks. Originally, proofreading meant reading the physical page proofs, to make sure that everything was ready for print. Now it is also your opportunity to check digital files for any final problems and oversights and catch any grammatical errors or errors that may have been accidentally introduced during a previous round of corrections.

Book Doctors

Book doctors occupy a space between developmental editors and manuscript appraisers. They work with writers to take existing material and drastically reshape it into a workable manuscript. It's different from a structural or developmental edit because the book doctor will not only identify problem areas, but will implement the solution, which can result in them rewriting portions of the manuscript.

A good book doctor will make the process a collaboration, so at the end of the day, the author still feels ownership of that project.

Be aware that there is some overlap of services between book doctoring, manuscript appraisal, and content editing. Ask the service provider for a description of what they do to be sure of what you're getting.

WHAT TO LOOK FOR IN AN EDITOR

Compatible Styles

Editing requires a close working relationship between the author and the editor, and it's important to find one who meshes well with your style, personality, and writing process. You won't always agree with your editor's advice, but having a deep level of compatibility minimizes friction and allows for a synergy that will bring out the very best in your work.

Samples

Ideally, your prospective editor will offer to edit a short sample of your writing to determine if you are a good match for each other, and so you can see their work firsthand. This is an important part of gauging compatibility, and is strongly advised before committing to the full editing process.

A sample edit will give you insight into the editor's style and process, and it will allow you to see what you'll receive for your money. Additionally, it gives the editor a better sense of the extent of the editing needed, so they can provide a more accurate estimate.

The length of the sample will vary, and some editors will provide this for free while others charge a standard or discounted rate for this step.

Partial Edits

If you're unsure of how much editing your work will require, consider hiring an editor for a partial edit of your work. In editing a few chapters of your work, your editor can spotlight areas that are a consistent problem for you. For example, you may have a pet phrase that creeps into your work too often, or a penchant for the passive voice.

Once a partial edit reveals these issues, you can perform another round of self-editing to clean up the known problems. Then you can go back to the editor with a cleaner manuscript that requires less work, saving you money.

Genre and Subject

Aside from personality and style, you'll also want to select an editor who is comfortable working in your genre and who has substantial experience with it. Experience brings an understanding of the nuances of a particular genre that goes far beyond technical competence, and it's especially vital in content editing.

Similarly, if your work involves a region, time, or subject that requires specialized knowledge, it may be helpful if your editor is already well versed in its conventions, quirks, idiom, and dialect.

Multiple Rounds of Editing

Find out whether your editor offers multiple rounds of edits at a discounted rate, or just a single pass. For proofreading and copyediting, a single pass may be sufficient, but developmental/content editing tends to be an iterative process requiring several rounds.

Availability

Finally, be aware that editing can be a time-consuming process, and popular editors may have a waiting list. Don't leave this step for the last-minute stages of your publishing process; research and book your editor in advance whenever possible.

9

DESIGN SERVICES

With the text of your book nearing completion, you'll begin to turn your attention to presentation. On the outside, your cover design will package your book so as to attract your target audience. On the inside, formatting styles your text to create a professional and pleasant reading experience.

COVER DESIGN

Your book's cover is arguably the most vital marketing tool at your disposal. It is the first impression readers will have of your book and your authorial brand.

Consider that thousands of titles are added to online retailers *every day*, all of them vying for customers' attention. A cover that looks good, represents your story, and is of a professional quality is essential in this increasingly competitive market. Finding a cover design artist willing to work with you to ensure that these three criteria are met is therefore equally important.

Identifying Your Design Needs

Do you want a specific look that brands all your books? Similar covers for particular series? Imagery that matches other covers in your genre? Or do you want to be more creative, and do something different?

Knowing in advance what you want for your cover can help create smooth interactions with your designer. However, being too rigid in your specifications can cramp the designer's style, potentially depriving you of that creative flair that makes an exceptional, unique cover. Remember that you're hiring a cover designer not only for their technical competence, but for their artistry as well.

Design trends surge into prominence and fade into clichés, so you'll want to get a feel for what's working well in your genre. Browse through the top-selling titles in your genre on Amazon, and note which covers you find especially eye-catching, and which ones leave you cold. Cover designers may ask you for examples of covers you like, and these examples can be helpful in pinning down the general approach you're looking for.

Technical Considerations

Investigate the technical requirements of the services you'll use. For example, online retailers such as Amazon display tiny thumbnail images of your cover. If your cover image is unrecognizable at this small size, you will lose potential sales. These technical considerations may affect your choice of subject or presentation on the cover. Your cover designer will need to know what trim size you've chosen —the dimensions of your book—before undertaking a project.

Identify your goals and requirements before approaching a designer and deepening the conversation.

Finding a Cover Designer

Word-of-mouth referrals are useful starting points for finding a good cover designer, but you'll still need to do your homework. What works for one author's book may not be right for another's, and authors may not be aware of best practices for design.

Nonetheless, these referrals are worth investigating, as a happy client is one indicator of an excellent service provider.

While researching your genre's trends and tropes, you may find a cover of exceptional beauty. Look for the designer credits on the back cover or the copyright page, as you might want to hire the artist for your own book.

Versatility

A skilled cover designer demonstrates a wide range of styles and mood in their work. Look through your prospective designer's portfolio. Do the covers all look the same? Do they reuse the same stock photos, fonts, or graphic elements?

With the absolutely massive competition facing any new release, your cover will need to stand out from the crowd. A designer who displays only repetitive cookie-cutter designs may not have the artistic range needed for the arresting, beautiful cover your book deserves.

Source Files

Some cover designers will provide the source files for the cover on request, so that you or another designer can make minor adjustments in the future. This is a valuable perk that is by no means standard, but it can be extremely helpful if the trim size, length, or other details of your book change in the future and the original designer is unavailable.

Pricing

Design services can vary widely in price and billing approach. Some charge by the hour, some assess fees based on the complexity and difficulty of the work, and some charge a flat fee (as low as $99 for a "pre-made" cover, with custom covers averaging $425).

Regardless of the pricing model, more expensive does not always mean better. Comparison shop to find high quality at reasonable prices.

A majority of cover designers work from stock photos to reduce costs and labor, but be aware that transforming a stock photo into a work of art can still be a laborious process requiring significant skill. Expect to pay substantially more for bespoke photography and custom illustrations.

Designing Your Own Cover

It may be tempting to cut corners by designing your own cover, especially if you have some artistic talent. Before you consider this approach, think long and hard on these facts:

1. A professional cover is one of the most important factors in the sales success of your book.
2. Design demands more than talent, or familiarity with Photoshop. It requires a solid grasp of layout, composition, color psychology, typography, the conventions of genre, and other facets of illustration.
3. Book cover design in particular involves technical considerations that go beyond the art. What looks good on a full-size canvas may not work as a tiny Amazon thumbnail. What works well as a striking piece of standalone art or photography may not work as a commercial sales tool.

If you have a strong professional background in graphic design, and have done the extensive research into the specific requirements of cover design, DIY design may be a viable option. Most authors, however, would be strongly advised to seek a professional designer rather than risk an ineffective or amateurish cover that will doom their book to poor sales.

Be especially wary of online "cover generators" and templates. These seldom produce an appealing design, and in the hands of an amateur, they are capable of producing monstrous eyesores.

Legal Considerations

Whether you choose to get a cover image from a design service or design your own cover, you should familiarize yourself with the legal issues surrounding copyrights and licensing for any images or fonts used. You will find valuable information on these topics in the Author Advice Centre (selfpublishingadvice.org), and in *The Self-Publisher's Legal Handbook*, the highly recommended book by our legal advisor, Helen Sedwick.

Before paying or signing a contract with a cover designer, be sure you know who owns the rights to the design, and how the cover can be used by both parties. Bear in mind that stock photo services often place restrictions on the number of copies that may be printed. Your cover designer should be able to provide you with these details.

MANUSCRIPT CONVERSION

Manuscript conversion is simply taking one form of your manuscript —be it in DOC/DOCX, RTF, PDF, or even a physical copy of a back-list title—and converting it into a digital format that is ready for ebook or print-on-demand (POD) production.

With the exception of converting a physical book into an editable file, manuscript conversion is largely automated, and fairly easy with the right tools.

Basic manuscript conversion is available for free or at a low cost from a variety of providers. For example:

- Kindle Direct Publishing will convert your manuscript at no charge.
- PublishDrive offers a sleek and free ebook conversion utility.
- StreetLib provides a free manuscript converter, StreetLib Write, that will export an EPUB file.
- Draft2Digital provides free ebook and print manuscript conversion that can be used anywhere.

Paid services and formatting software may include manuscript conversion features as well:

- Scrivener, an immensely popular word processor designed for authors, can import your manuscript and export to a variety of formats.
- Anthemion Jutoh is a low-cost, full-featured ebook editor that can produce EPUB, MOBI, and other formats.
- Recent versions of Adobe InDesign can export your manuscript to EPUB format.
- Vellum is an extremely popular formatting suite that is currently only available to Mac users.

These services are capable of producing a sales-ready ebook with no further work needed, so long as you have a clean and professionally edited manuscript that you have set up properly. Nonetheless, many authors choose to hire a formatter to take their books to the next level, not only converting the manuscript, but generating a clean, lightweight, and beautiful interior.

Formatting Services

Formatting is the process of laying out your manuscript for print or ebook production. Formatting has significant overlap with manuscript conversion, but usually involves a more rigorous process that includes layout, chapter headings, indentation, optimization of illustrations and other images, and so on.

Print books will faithfully reproduce the appearance of your manuscript, and generally require more effort to establish a consistent style. Ebooks, on the other hand, have greater limitations in style, fonts, and layout, and so formatting ebooks is as much a matter of stripping away unnecessary formatting as imparting new styles.

Both ebooks and print books benefit from professional formatting.

Formatting may be offered as an à la carte service, or as part of a package of publishing services. Regardless, you should look for service providers who have an established presence on the web and a solid track record. Authors are advised to be wary of sites such as Fiverr, where fly-by-night operators often congregate.

The best indication of a formatter's quality is their past work. Ask for examples of books the formatter has worked on, so you can judge the quality firsthand.

Ask what services your formatter provides. At the minimum, a formatter will remove redundant whitespace, develop an appealing and easy-to-read style, and apply it consistently throughout your book. Images such as tables, graphic chapter headings, fleurons and dividers, and illustrations may incur additional fees. Let your formatter know if these elements are present in your book, and in what quantities.

Do-It-Yourself Formatting

There are several programs available to help authors format and lay out their books for a variety of purposes. These span a wide range of prices and technical expertise, so it's important to know what you'll need for your particular projects and goals.

If you write crime thrillers, you're not likely to need a program with functionality for designing pages with lots of graphics, and so the default capabilities of Scrivener or Word may be sufficient. But if you are preparing a cookbook, a children's book, or other illustrated book, a high-end package like Adobe InDesign may be the better investment for you despite its steep price and learning curve.

Authors should weigh the effort and expense of these programs against the convenience of hiring a professional formatter.

10

PRODUCTION SERVICES

Once an ebook has been formatted, production is virtually complete as you now have a digital file ready to distribute to your readers. Print, on the other hand, involves the manufacture, storage, and delivery of the book, all of which must be arranged for sales to take place. Audiobooks, too, have their own production path that differs from other formats.

PRINT PRODUCTION

Production can be a daunting task for a first-time self-publishing author. Once you get past the jargon, though, some simple tools and services can make it a much more manageable task.

Depending on what your goals are, the worth of production services varies. The first time, it helps to have someone there who will take the lead on the process and help you understand each step, but you may find that it's more fitting for you to do it yourself in the future.

Print-on-Demand

The majority of authors rely on print-on-demand production for their books. This method has slightly higher per-unit costs than traditional printing methods such as offset printing. However, it avoids the need for massive print runs to maintain stock and the warehousing to store it. Further, each book is printed as needed, so any errors found in a manuscript can be corrected almost instantly.

Amazon's KDP and IngramSpark are the front-runners for print-on-demand production, both for independent authors and for self-publishing services. These two companies utilize a worldwide network of printers to rapidly produce individual copies of books, as needed, and deliver them to a distribution center.

Each company has its own advantages. Using KDP allows authors access to Amazon's incomparably huge customer base, with the added bonus of rapid fulfillment for those customers. IngramSpark offers superior international fulfillment and more flexible options for distribution to brick-and-mortar bookstores or libraries.

It is possible to use both services simultaneously, and ALLi highly recommends this two-pronged approach for authors seeking global distribution plus faster fulfillment for Amazon customers.

Offset and Specialty Printing

Historically, offset printing has been the preferred method for large publishers due to economies of scale. Most indie authors will find print-on-demand to be more forgiving, more affordable, and a better fit for online sales, but offset printing remains a viable alternative— and the only option in some cases.

Offset printing may be required for books over 800 pages; books with odd trim sizes; books with unusual paper; and art or photography books that require higher print fidelity.

If you're considering this option, you will need to prepare in advance. Offset printing is carried out in large runs of hundreds or thousands of books at a time, and those books will need to be shipped and stored at the author's expense. Learn in advance about the different printing options available to you, and the typical cost of each.

You will need to make a realistic assessment of the risk and reward: offset printing creates significant savings in the per-unit cost of the books, but that's only if the books sell. Any errors in the manuscript will be costly to fix.

Print-on-demand is therefore the safer and more flexible option for most authors.

AUDIOBOOK PRODUCTION

Audiobooks are a popular format, and even the preferred format for many readers. The cost of production can be daunting, however. Audiobook production is usually billed by the *finished hour*, meaning the total work required to produce one hour of the final product. Costs may run upwards of $250 per finished hour, with the average audiobook weighing in around 10 hours in length.

Those fees may seem high, but consider that it takes 6 to 8 hours of narration and editing to produce one finished hour of audiobook, and so that 10-hour audiobook may require 60 to 80 hours of actual production.

It is very difficult to match the quality of professional audio production at home. Narration is a deceptively difficult profession, one that requires a good deal more than an appealing voice and clear diction. It requires specialized equipment, editing software, and on-the-job experience. And it requires time, a commodity that's often in short supply for indie authors.

Indie authors who want to record their own audio should invest in a high-end audio setup and a dedicated recording "studio" environment. Under no circumstances should you attempt to produce an audiobook with a cheap microphone headset, or worse, with text-to-speech software. The first will generate poor quality that is unlikely to pass retailer requirements, and the latter will sound alien and robotic. (Even for science fiction, that's not a recipe for success.)

Most authors rely on an audiobook producer such as Amazon-owned ACX, ListenUp Audio, Author's Republic, or Findaway Voices to handle this process. These services help pair authors and narrators to create high-quality audiobooks.

Authors using these services will identify their project and what qualities they're seeking in a narrator—vocal quality, gender, age, accent, special dialects, and so on. Some services let the author browse through the available narrators, listening to samples of their work. Others set up auditions with a selection of likely candidates, and the author chooses their favorite. Still others allow you to upload a sample of your manuscript, which interested narrators will audition for by providing a brief recording of your work.

Payment generally takes one of two forms:

Payment Upfront

The author and narrator (or author and service) agree on a per-finished-hour rate. If the author can afford the initial investment, this is often the preferred method of compensation. It involves less risk for the narrator, and after the distributor's fees, all subsequent profit from the audiobook belongs to the author, for the life of the audiobook.

Payment Split

The author and narrator split all profits from the audiobook according to a given percentage. This kind of partnership puts a heavy burden of risk on the narrator, because the narrator is investing many hours of work with no guarantee that the audiobook will sell. It's more common among newer narrators trying to build their experience, and it can be a great alternative for cash-strapped authors. However, because of the risk involved, narrators may be unwilling to consider this option without evidence of good sales and good reviews for the author's books.

Comparison shopping is vital for audiobook production. Shop

around to find the service with the best fit for your goals, and then within that service to find the best narrator for your audiobook.

METADATA

Metadata refers to the details of the book outside of its actual text: its title, author, publisher, page count, language, price, publication date, and much more.

There are various systems to catalogue and track this information, but in retail environments, the ISBN is king.

What is an ISBN?

ISBN stands for International Standard Book Number, and each component of that name is important. It is **internationally** recognized; it is a **standard** format used across many different platforms and companies; and it is specific to **books**.

An ISBN is used to identify and track your book through complex distribution chains so that interested parties can request and order it. It is unique not only to your book, but to a specific format, language, and edition of that book. For example, a hardcover edition of a book will have its own identifier separate from the paperback, ebook, or audiobook versions. This allows retailers to avoid confusion and deliver the precise product a customer requests.

The Need for ISBNs

The need to purchase ISBNs is a controversial topic in the indie community. Proponents argue that it is a necessary part of professional book production, one that provides a globally recognized, enduring, and standardized means of identifying and cataloging your books. Opponents object to the cost, and question the need for direct ownership when retailer-specific ISBNs are available at a discount on many retail platforms. And on some platforms, such as Amazon, internal identifiers may take the place of an ISBN.

Obtaining an ISBN

Each country has a registrar responsible for assigning ISBNs to books. In some countries, ISBNs are a function of a government agency, which may distribute them for free or at a low cost. In others, ISBNs are managed by an appointed registrar who sells registrations, sometimes for a substantial fee. In the US, the appointed registrar for ISBNs is R.R. Bowker; in the UK, it is Nielsen Book. These registrars are the sole provider of ISBNs in their respective countries.

However, publishers and retailers may act as resellers, purchasing large blocks of numbers at a discount and then reselling them to clients. In this case, the reseller remains the owner of the registration, and the only access the author will have to the ISBN metadata is through that reseller.

ALLi advice is to purchase your own ISBNs directly from your national registrar, so that you are the official owner of that registration. An ISBN identifies you to all interested parties—bookstores, libraries, catalogues—as the publisher of your book, now and in the future. Owning your ISBN registration leaves you in control of that data, allowing you to make changes at any time.

In contrast, purchasing a discounted ISBN from a reseller strips you of that control. You will be unable to use that ISBN with other retailers or distributors, and should the reseller go out of business or divest itself of its publishing arm, you may be left with no way to update your data.

Most paid registrars offer significant discounts for bulk purchases of ISBNs. It is advisable to purchase a block of ISBNs to cover all of the formats you might conceivably produce in the future.

Although some use "barcode" and "ISBN" interchangeably, these are two different concepts. While you will likely have to pay for an ISBN registration, the barcode is simply a representation of that number. Do not pay for barcode representations of an ISBN; there are many online tools that provide this utility at no charge.

11

DISTRIBUTION SERVICES

Distribution refers to the process and logistics of actually getting your book to the consumer. There is a myriad of services and platforms available to put your work in the hands of readers. Each has pros and cons, depending on your needs.

- Are you a new author seeking to quickly grow your reader audience?
- Are you seeking expanded distribution into new markets worldwide?
- Are you planning to market an ebook only, or a variety of editions such as paperback, hardcover, ebook?
- Are you committed to pushing for distribution to brick-and-mortar bookstores, or will you focus exclusively on the lucrative online market?
- Will you want your book to be available in libraries? What royalties will you sacrifice for that exposure?

These are all questions you will need to examine before deciding on a distribution strategy. For now, it's helpful to have a general understanding of the types of distribution available to authors.

What is a Distributor?

A distributor, in its most general sense, is any company that provides products to retailers or libraries instead of directly to consumers. Distributors handle the logistics of shipping and delivery, manage billing on the author's behalf, and in some cases act as the sole vendor from which retailers can obtain your book.

Many companies act as both publishers and distributors, producing books as well as making them available to various retail venues. However, the majority of these distributors are actually *wholesalers*, passive suppliers who only respond to book orders, as opposed to active distributors who have a sales team dedicated to placing books with retailers.

Although the term "distributor" is used to refer to both types of service, understanding the distinction between a passive wholesaler and an active, sales-oriented distributor is crucial.

What is an Aggregator?

An aggregator is a service that provides books to multiple distributors, giving authors access to potentially thousands of retailers from a single point of entry. It's a great way to widen your books' availability without incurring the overhead of dealing directly with a multitude of services.

Aggregators are most common in ebook distribution, as the electronic format is particularly well suited to this kind of arrangement. Authors upload their ebook file (or a manuscript to be converted), and then select the networks and retailers they wish to distribute their book to.

Aggregators may charge a flat fee or a share of royalties (typically 10% of the sales price) for this service.

CHOOSING YOUR EBOOK DISTRIBUTION NETWORKS

In choosing your ebook distribution strategy, you will first need to consider which venues offer advantages for signing up directly, and whether those benefits outweigh the convenience of using an aggregator.

Signing up directly for Amazon's KDP is relatively easy, grants you full and immediate control over your books, and gives you access to powerful marketing tools such as the Amazon Marketing Services (AMS) advertising platform and KDP Select's Countdown Deals for ebooks. Because KDP is so tightly integrated with Amazon's retail operations, there is little benefit to using an aggregator or outside distributor to reach Amazon shoppers.

If you are comfortable with managing multiple accounts and navigating the online interfaces of the major retailers, you may also wish to sign up directly with Barnes & Noble, Kobo, and iTunes (which requires you to use a Mac). Direct access to these sellers maximizes control over your ebooks and provides slightly higher royalties.

For the countless remaining retailers, the centralized management of aggregators is a blessing to any indie author, and well worth the small cut of the royalties charged by these services.

Avoid ebook distribution services that try to lock you into exclusive contracts. Most ebook aggregators do not require exclusive agreements, and there is great benefit in being able to leverage the strengths and scope of multiple aggregators. If you do use multiple aggregators, you may need to compare their distribution channels to avoid overlaps.

CHOOSING YOUR PRINT DISTRIBUTION NETWORKS

Distribution to Online Retailers

Distribution to online retailers is a reasonably straightforward proposition if you're using print-on-demand production. Most of your sales will come from online retailers, and the two largest print-on-demand companies serving that market are Amazon and IngramSpark.

Neither requires an exclusive agreement, and as we discussed earlier, there are strong advantages to using both of these companies together for distribution. To do so, you would opt out of Amazon's Expanded Distribution program, and use Amazon to serve only its own customers. IngramSpark distribution can then be used to serve the other venues in its huge distribution network.

You can order books from either service at cost for your own use, which allows you to maintain a personal stock for book signings, consignments, or direct-to-consumer website sales.

Distribution to Brick-and-Mortar Stores

Although distributing your book to online sellers is fairly simple, distributing your print book to physical bookstores presents additional complications.

First, there's the matter of persuading these retailers to carry your book. Employing a service that boasts of "tens of thousands" of retailers and libraries in their distribution network will not ensure that your book is carried by those retailers; it only ensures that a retailer who *asks to purchase that book* has the option to do so. Few retailers will be interested in ordering and stocking a fairly obscure book. It takes time to build up your authorial presence, and sales, so unless you have a blockbuster debut, finding retailers to carry your book can be a significant challenge.

Second, there's the matter of wholesale discounting. Physical bookstores expect a wholesale discount, typically 55%, which enables them to sell the books for a profit at list prices. This is the industry standard for brick-and-mortar sales, and it will reduce your profits.

Finally, bookstores will expect the ability to return unsold books for a refund. This incurs some uncertainty for the indie author, as a sale to a bookstore is not necessarily final. It also may result in losses: depending on the agreement, the author can be liable for shipping costs to return unwanted books, or the author can specify that returned books be destroyed, the cost of which comes out of the author's pocket.

Remember that listing your book with a distributor does not guarantee that retailers will carry it. It only makes the option available to those who know about it, and wish to stock the book.

Making your book known to these retailers—and the readers they serve—is the goal of the next stage of publishing: marketing and promotion.

Libraries

One other service that deserves a special mention is low-tech and has been around a long time: libraries. Unlike bookstores, the people who work at libraries know books inside out. Many of them treat authors like rock stars. And they talk to readers all day long.

They are arguably the most important influencers in the book ecosystem. And they do an amazing job for the reading and writing community.

We have a section on how to get your book into libraries in our guide *Opening Up to Indie Authors*. Here our focus is the many services now stepping up to provide a link between your publishing platform and the ebook library infrastructure—mostly in the US, where there are thousands of libraries with the facility to loan ebooks.

Libraries are keen to offer self-published books, but with over 600,000 indie titles published every year in the US alone, librarians don't have the time or resources to filter the good from the bad.

Librarians also face tight budgetary constraints. Traditionally, mainstream publishers have sold print copies to libraries at a high markup (often five to ten times the price paid by consumers). After the book is checked out 20 or 30 times, it may need to be replaced.

Absurdly, this print model has been carried over into the digital age, with Digital Rights Management installed in the ebooks purchased by libraries, which both limits the number of individual checkouts and requires a "copy" to be repurchased after an overall number of loans or a preset period.

Getting Your Books into Libraries

In addition to wholesalers who make books available for purchase, there are a few distributors that specialize in connecting independent authors to the growing library ebook system. The most notable of these are SELF-e, OverDrive, and Bibliotheca.

It's important to remember that library ebook loans are part of an emergent sector. There is no perfect system for this evolving venue, so authors will need to evaluate each to determine which most closely aligns with their needs and philosophy.

OverDrive

OverDrive is the world's largest library ebook platform. It offers a procurement and checkout system for over 40,000 public libraries and schools around the world. OverDrive was acquired in 2015 by Rakuten, which also owns Kobo.

Ebooks are supplied via a publishing platform such as Smashwords, PublishDrive, or Draft2Digital to library databases, where librarians decide which titles to acquire.

The curation process varies depending on the platform. Matador uses NetGalley to connect with librarians; Smashwords titles are curated for quality and library requirements, and the titles that pass are then made available to librarians.

Authors are compensated, and can set custom library prices through their ebook distributor's dashboard. They then earn 45% of that amount for each title sold to a library.

Pros:

- Authors can set price and get paid for library sales
- Global (but US-skewed)
- User-friendly app, Libby, offers book searching and sampling

Cons:

- No support for titles priced at $1.99 or lower
- Some platforms curate based on previous visibility and retail success
- Favors assisted publishing platforms

Bibliotheca

Bibliotheca's digital lending platform is called cloudLibrary, and it is utilized by more than 30,000 libraries worldwide.

Ebooks are supplied through distributors and publishing platforms. There is minimal curation, mostly for technical aspects.

Authors are paid through one of two models. The "standard" library model mimics physical books: libraries purchase a single copy, which can be loaned out to only one patron at a time. Authors typically receive three times the list price, but as a one-time transaction, much like a retail sale.

In the multiple loan model, also known as the "cost-per-checkout" or "pay-per-use" model, libraries can loan ebooks from their collection to multiple patrons simultaneously, and the library pays one tenth of the list price per loan.

Pros:

- Authors can choose from standard or multiple loan models
- Authors can set prices and receive ongoing revenue from loans
- Global (but US-skewed)
- cloudLibrary offers user-friendly features like parental passwords, multi-device sync, and support for ten languages

Cons:

- Access through publishing platforms only, which may take a percentage of each sale

SELF-e

At the author level, SELF-e is built around the permafree marketing concept, which values long-term author exposure over short-term income.

Ebooks are vetted by *Library Journal*, the national publication for the library community. If accepted, they are displayed to librarians via BiblioBoard's loan and acquisition system, which, it's claimed, is used by around 2,700 libraries and reaches 30 million patrons. SELF-e is effectively a partnership between BiblioBoard and Library Journal.

SELF-e has attracted criticism over its business model, which charges libraries to acquire titles but offers no royalty to authors. There are serious questions over the past relationship between SELF-e's parent company, Library Journal, and the controversial vanity press Author Solutions. And ALLi also raised concerns over SELF-e's connection to Library Journal's "2015 Self-published Ebook Awards," urging changes to some ambiguous terms and conditions, especially around "irrevocable" rights and other atypical language.

SELF-e operates on two tiers. The author submits their book, via the Library Journal system. If selected, it's made available to loan via "Library Journal SELF-e Select," which is offered to US libraries nationwide.

If the book isn't selected, then it's deferred to the "Statewide Indie Anthology," and made available via the local library system on a state-by-state basis.

SELF-e is focused on discovery, and authors are not compensated. According to Library Journal's Patron Profiles report, "over 50 percent of all library users go on to purchase ebooks by an author they were introduced to in a library."

Pros:

- Not restricted to US authors
- Quick and easy submission
- Greater potential for selection due to two-tier system

Cons:

- No author payment
- Ethical concerns over connection to Author Solutions
- No dedicated app

The Bottom Line

It's important for authors to recognize that these three services are not like for like. They offer different options depending on territory, career priorities, and marketing strategy.

Authors must have a clear sense of what they hope to achieve from their book's availability in a library system and choose accordingly.

SELF-e, for example, is not a sales solution with paid revenue. It's a curated discovery channel and if, as an author, you have an issue with offering free content to a broader readership—perhaps out of concerns over sales cannibalization—then SELF-e is not for you.

But, aside from concerns over relationships with businesses like Author Solutions, it is a potential path for independent authors to gain access to an area traditionally ring-fenced by the big publishers.

As with all aspects of self-publishing, it's crucial to seek professional help from service providers and demand the highest possible standards to ensure your books are indistinguishable from those produced by traditional publishers.

Whatever the methods of curation, libraries will be more prepared to take a risk on self-published titles over traditional, because the pricing tends to be lower, but only if the book looks professional and credible.

Although we are obviously sensitive to moral issues around author payment and business ethics, the current routes for access to libraries are more about visibility than bank balance. At the moment, there isn't a huge amount of money in the library market, so smart authors should select a solution they're comfortable with and use it as part of a longer-term strategy of increasing their profile.

Regardless of which approach an author chooses, libraries remain an avenue for broader exposure that shouldn't be ignored, especially if library users go on to purchase ebooks by an author they were introduced to in a library.

"Library patrons do purchase books," says Smashwords' Mark Coker. "That's because libraries are engines of discovery."

12

MARKETING SERVICES

The access to readers that the self-publishing revolution has brought has been an amazing boon to authors, but it has also introduced new challenges. Chief among these is discoverability.

Thousands of titles enter the market *each day*. The explosive growth of the number of books available to readers has created an incredibly crowded field in which most titles rapidly disappear into obscurity. Surfacing your book and bringing it to the attention of readers is one of the most difficult tasks any indie author faces.

In this Marketing section and the next (Promotion), we'll look at some of the options for publicizing you and your books, as well as the many snares that lie in wait to trap the unwary author.

Hiring a service to help you market and promote your book—and you—is tricky. We've long wished at ALLi that book marketers and PR agencies would offer their services on results-based payment. There is no other service where the customer is told: the bill is thousands of pounds and I may get you no return on your investment.

There is no other service where you are more vulnerable to having your dreams of success exploited. Writer beware!

If you decide to outsource your marketing ensure your chosen service has experience marketing books in your genre. Check their LinkedIn. Google them, and check out the works they've edited along with any reviews or testimonials.

No author should outsource marketing until they know what works for them and their books. Before signing anyone, create a clear marketing plan so your marketing agent or publicist knows your goals.

First-time authors, for example, might just want to get readers for their book and not be overly focussed on sales or income. A marketer with book giveaway campaigns who can demonstrate the ability to deliver a certain amount of new readers. Or if you're trying to increase your social media presence, hire someone with proven experience in doing this. These things are easy to check.

Also come up with a payment plan.

EFFECTIVE BOOK MARKETING

Do take note of the distinction between marketing and promotion. Book marketing goes beyond limited-time promotions. It encompasses the full scope of what we at ALLi think of as "reaching readers." Anything that gives readers information about you or your books, gets readers interested in you, and attracts notice is marketing.

This includes your book's cover, back cover blurb, pricing, store placement, website, promotional offers, social media, word of mouth, publicity, and more. Marketing is ongoing.

Promotion, however, is time-based. It generally relates to a specific book, and is an awareness project, or special offer, designed to increase sales of a particular title.

As with any aspect of publishing, you can hire a service to assist with marketing and promotion. Companies can help to connect you with readers, and apply their experience to your specific needs. A vast number of new companies have arisen in recent times, offering everything from old-style press releases to digital click campaigns.

Good Marketing Services Offer Support

The reason most authors choose a paid service is that they are daunted by the thought of marketing and promoting their books. Yet many services offering "marketing" are offering no more than leaflets, business cards, a website, or showing an author how to set up a social media account.

Printed bookmarks, posters, business cards and the like are not marketing services; they are materials. If this is all that is being offered by your service, you are effectively on your own when it comes to marketing and promoting your book.

Good marketing and promotion services bring more to the table than this. They work with the author to introduce fresh ideas and suggestions, as well as being willing to take the author's own ideas on board. They plan and implement strategy over a period of several months. They know what strategies work for books in a particular genre.

The service should not just be using the author's own provided contact list. It should possess its own lists of press and bloggers, and other tools and resources. A "press release" should see the provider sending targeted information to particular journalists and bloggers, not a blanket, standard email.

And so on. Ask specifically about services that take time (your most precious asset) and distinguish these from materials.

Know Your Strengths and Weaknesses

When you put together a marketing plan, you want to keep in mind what existing platforms you might already have. A dedicated following from previous books? An author website? An engaged social media following? Contacts with press or reader blogs? These can be leveraged to amplify your marketing efforts.

Also look at what areas you can improve to help bolster sales and visibility. Marketing means looking at how you're getting readers to discover you and your work. Will you be a part of a library program that doesn't necessarily boost sales, but increases discoverability? Can you write guest entries for blogs that would appeal to your target market? Are you signed up for social networking sites like Twitter and using an author page on Facebook?

MARKETING METHODS

Not every marketing tactic is right for every writer or market, so when you create your marketing plan—or hire a service provider to create one for you—take note of what other successful authors in your field are doing, and also what they've tried and left behind.

Public Relations: PR

Traditional PR methods are still viable in today's digital age. Targeted, personal press releases, interviews, and reviews in print publications are all valid ways of reaching readers and expanding awareness of books. The mode may have changed—reaching out independently as opposed to through an agent or publisher—but the goal is still the same: to get the word about your work out to prospective readers.

Whereas promotions focus on limited-time sales opportunities for readers, discounting, and suchlike, PR is more peer-oriented, looking to gain reviews, blog tours, and book signings, together with ongoing efforts like social media engagement.

It's important to have a solid plan for bringing your book out with a bang, but also to schedule time to do ongoing marketing that will keep readers interested. An author's appeal is rarely just their books; it's also their life, character, habits, and process. In an atmosphere where consumers are constantly bombarded with advertisements, if you only pop up when you want them to buy your books, you'll be out of sight—and out of mind—before you can say "My new book..."

If this is a part of the process you'd rather take a back seat on, PR services can help spread awareness of your work while keeping you in the reader's eye.

When evaluating a PR service, there are two primary factors to consider. Do they understand your needs and expectations? And, can they deliver what they promise?

The first is vital to a good working relationship. The purpose of hiring a PR firm is to ease the burden of those tasks, but a firm with different expectations may wind up increasing that burden, pushing you to engage in activities and schedules you're unable or unwilling to commit to. Good communication is essential from the start, so be forthright about what you're looking for, and what you're willing to put into the campaign.

The second can be more difficult to assess, and will require careful investigation. The best indication of how a PR firm will deliver on its promises is its past performance. Search for the company's project. Is there evidence of past success? A PR company whose work is invisible on the internet may not be doing much to promote its clients.

REVIEWS

It's important to understand the distinction between editorial reviews and customer reviews, because the rules governing them differ greatly.

Customer Reviews

Customer reviews are meant to express the opinions of consumers, free of incentives or other manipulation. These are the comments you find on retail sites and review sites like Yelp. Positive reviews provide valuable reassurance to consumers who are trying to decide whether to make a purchase.

Relatively few consumers leave reviews, and it can be difficult for new authors to amass positive comments and ratings on retail sites. That scarcity has given rise to various services designed to get customer reviews. But many of these services are unethical, and may contravene retailer rules. That could lead to your reviews being stripped in the best case, and your account suspended in the worst.

Customer reviews should always be organic. Exchanging money, discounts, or other incentives for a review is unethical, as it deceives consumers who believe they're reading a peer's unbiased opinion. Authors should never purchase customer reviews in this way.

However, there is a notable exception: advance review copies (ARCs), free copies of the book given to reviewers. This is a long-standing practice in the industry, and is not considered an incentive valuable enough to distort the reviewer's opinion.

Additionally, there are some services that act as an intermediary between reviewers and the author. The author may appear to "buy reviews" from the service, but if the service is simply distributing ARCs on behalf of the author, and not attempting to influence the content of the review, this is perfectly acceptable. But if the service is essentially bribing reviewers with gifts, coupons, sweepstakes entries, redeemable points, or other incentives, an author using that service is sailing into murky waters.

An author purchasing fraudulent reviews may face condemnation and disciplinary action by retailers when caught, so be sure you know exactly how a review service is obtaining those reviews. Avoid any company with even a hint of unethical conduct.

Editorial Reviews

Editorial reviews occupy a different space—both literally and figuratively—than customer reviews. While customer reviews provide the opinion of shoppers' peers as social proof, editorial reviewers rely on reputation and experience to lend authority to their words, and are usually kept distinct from customer reviews.

Companies such as Kirkus, Foreword Reviews, Chanticleer Reviews, and BlueInk Review stand out in this field. These companies have earned the trust of readers with a history of unbiased reviews and good practices. Because editorial reviews are clearly identified as such, and because these companies maintain a firewall between the reviewers and any compensation from the author, there is no conflict of interest in their being paid.

The value of an editorial review is often debated. A glowing review from a well-known source may persuade consumers, but will the average reader recognize an editorial reviewer as an authority? Empirically, there is little evidence that an editorial review increases sales, and certainly not to the extent that an author will recoup the cost of a high-end review service. It's an investment without a clear return, although it may contribute to the overall impression your book makes on shoppers.

If you choose to purchase an editorial review, keep in mind that it's an unbiased review, so there is no guarantee that it will be positive. While most services give you the option to suppress a negative review, there are no refunds if the reviewer posts a scathing assessment of your work.

AWARDS AND CONTESTS

Winning the right book award can be a catalyst for discovery, raising a self-published book out of obscurity, into the spotlight. How valuable that spotlight might be varies greatly but recognition from an esteemed panel of judges can increase a book's credibility, visibility, and marketability.

And it comes at a price. Contests can be expensive, especially if you are entering a number of them (entrance fees are usually between $75 and $200 USD per category). As well as the entry fee, there's the cost of shipping multiple copies of your printed book (ebooks generally upload for free).

A few contests offer cash prizes to top winners and the best awards give you usable feedback even if you don't win the main award.

However, some book awards are set up to make money for the organisers rather than recognizing the accomplishments of the entrants. There are very few non-profit contests and most contests produce good revenue for the organisers and sponsors, as well as increased traffic to their website as you spread the news of your win.

Some are not really competitions at all, but ploys to get you to use a vanity press or self-publishing service. If you are invited out of the blue to enter a "contest," It's more than likely one of those.

Some are even "pay-to-win" events, where you receive an "award" just for entering. Clearly this is bogus.

Here are the guiding principles by which the Watchdog Desk assesses rewards, which you can use yourself in assessing any awards program or contest that interests you.

1. The event exists to recognize talent, not to enrich the organizers.
Avoid events which are driven by excessive entry fees, marketing services to entrants, or selling merchandise like stickers and certificates.

2. Receiving an award is a significant achievement.
An event that hands out awards like Halloween candy dilutes the value of those awards, rendering them meaningless. Beware events that offer awards in dozens of categories. These are often schemes to maximize the number of winners in order to sell them stickers and other merchandise.

3. The judging process is transparent and clear.
Watch out for contests whose judging criteria and personnel are vague or undisclosed.

4. Prizes are appropriate and commensurate with the entry fees collected.
If a cash prize is offered, it should align with the size of the entry fee. "Exposure" is not an appropriate prize. Representation or publication are acceptable prizes, but only if offered by a reputable company without hidden fees.

5. Entrants are not required to forfeit key rights to their work.
Avoid contests with onerous terms, especially those which require the forfeiture of publishing rights without a termination clause. When in doubt, have an independent professional review the terms.

Awards for independent authors are not like the US National Book Award or UK's Booker Prize, giving a significant boost to sales and reputation, impact and influence. Few authors winning a self-publishing award notice any difference in book sales, no matter how hard they market their award.

That doesn't mean they are worthless. Award-winning ALLi authors agree that the awards reception, the medal, and the ability to put a sticker on their book are generally worth the entry fee. An award can give you an ego boost and, if you wish, you can display medals and stickers on your book, website, email signature, and wherever you want.

So enter any book award contest only after careful consideration and review of its reputation. Compare fees, and read about possible additional expenses if you win (such as purchasing stickers for your book or attending award ceremonies).

Read the fine print. Contact ALLi's Watchdog Desk and consult our Awards and Contests Ratings page. You'll find it at:

selfpublishingadvice.org/awards

DISCOUNTS AND PERMANENTLY FREE BOOKS

Discounted books more properly fall into the next chapter, which is about time-based special offers on a particular title. Marketing is more ongoing ways to draw attention to you and your work. Some authors use discounts and "permafree" in this way.

Offering the first book in a series for free, or at a heavily discounted price, is a common strategy. Readers tempted by the bargain may enjoy the book, and may go on to buy other books by that author at full price. This "loss leader" strategy can be very effective.

However, this mainstay of marketing strategy can be a slippery slope. Many authors have resorted to lowering the price of *all* of their books to better compete in an intensely crowded field. This sets a precedent of devaluing books that some experts feel can be harmful in the aggregate. Readers who grow accustomed to free and heavily discounted books may eschew regularly priced books, decimating author income.

Lowering the price of your book can stimulate sales, but that strategy can quickly reach over-saturation. It's the contrast with the normal list price that makes the promotion stand out as a deal, as something unusual and exciting.

Value your books appropriately, and reserve discounts for special promotions and incentives.

RESULTS ARE NOT GUARANTEED

It is notoriously difficult to quantify the success of individual marketing efforts. What works for one book may not work for another, and what works well on a first attempt may fizzle on a second.

No marketing approach is guaranteed.

However, some companies have a better history of successful marketing than others, and it is possible to separate the ones with the best chances of success from the ones that don't pass muster.

Always remain cognisant of the fact that marketing is a sector fraught with excessive hype, ineffective services, and outright fraud. Often, these failings are well hidden, because even while marketing companies may fail their clients, they can excel at promoting themselves.

Ultimately, the only true indicator of a marketing campaign's success is whether it produces measurable results. When evaluating marketing services of any kind, look to their clients. Are their books thriving, or languishing in obscurity? Did the clients recoup their expense?

Don't rely on cherry-picked testimonials, as these show only the comments the company wants you to see. For unvarnished assessments, look to independent reviews and firsthand feedback.

13

─────

PROMOTION SERVICES

Book promotions are limited-time incentives to attract the interest of readers. Utilizing limited-time markdowns, free-download days, giveaways, contests, and other events, authors can boost their revenue and bring in new readers. Those readers may go on to buy other titles now or in the future, or even become lifelong fans.

The efficacy of any given promotional strategy can't be guaranteed, but when used wisely, they can reap great benefits for an author. For example, it may seem counterintuitive to give a book away for free to raise revenue, but if you are releasing a new book in a series, having a period of free downloads for the first book can bring in new readers who would otherwise not have purchased the new book.

ADVERTISING

Finding the right platform, audience, and approach for an ad campaign can yield tremendous rewards, but this process comes with a steep learning curve and often involves extensive trial and error.

Amazon Marketing Services (AMS)

One of the hottest advertising platforms currently is Amazon Marketing Services, or AMS. AMS allows authors to display ads alongside Amazon search results, in a scrolling strip below product pages, in a panel below the buy button, and on Kindle lock screens.

AMS is a lucrative and increasingly competitive platform. It uses an auction system combined with obscure algorithms to determine which ads are shown. Users pay only when a customer clicks on the ad, which keeps costs down when experimenting with different strategies.

Ad setup is extremely simple, and can be tailored to any budget. However, the process of fine-tuning your ads to yield consistent returns is deceptively complex, and creating an ad that scales up will take time to master.

ALLi recommends Mark Dawson's online course Ads for Authors for anyone planning to use AMS. Learn more at selfpublishingformula.com.

Banner Ads

Banner ads on websites have fallen out of vogue thanks to more targeted ad systems like Google Ads. Banner ads typically have a low click-through rate and conversion rate when compared with other advertising platforms, and it can be difficult to achieve a positive return on your investment.

Before considering a purchase of a banner ad placement, familiarize yourself with the metrics of online advertising, and weigh the cost of the ad against its past performance. Cost effectiveness is crucial here, as the margin for a positive return on investment can be very slim.

Ebook Discovery Services

BookBub is considered the gold standard for ebook discovery services due to its massive audience, and its sterling track record of boosting sales and attracting new readers to your books.

Because of that success, BookBub commands a higher price than most ebook discovery services (the median price is $238 to promote a free book, and $1,198 to promote a book priced at $2.99).

It's also more difficult to secure a slot in the mailings. To be considered for a BookBub promotion, your book must be full-length; free or discounted by more than 50%; and it must not be available at a lower price within 90 days of the promotion.

If that describes your project, you can create an account to submit your book for consideration. An editorial team reviews submissions, and if you're accepted, you'll schedule a limited-time promotion on your selected retailers and pay for the ad. Once BookBub verifies you've discounted the book on the retailer website, it will run your ad.

It's definitely a more difficult process to go through than many other promotions, but the targeted marketing approach and reputation for promoting only the highest-quality books make it, in nearly every case, a worthwhile investment of time and money.

BookBub's competitors vary tremendously in price and quality, but a few stand out as worthwhile alternatives. Fussy Librarian, Book Barbarian, BookSends, and BargainBooksy have considerably smaller audiences than BookBub, but offer excellent value. These services are especially useful for "stacked" promotions, in which the author places several of these ads on the same day, or in rapid succession, to maximize the exposure for a promotion.

ALLi's Watchdog Desk publishes a detailed comparison of these services in our Self-Publishing Advice Centre: selfpublishingadvice.org.

Facebook Advertising

Facebook's advertising program has taken targeted marketing to a new level. You can specify the frequency with which your ads appear, the times of day, the geographic regions, and the demographics of your audience. You can target mobile users, desktop users, or both. You can display your ad only to users with a particular interest or lifestyle. And you can tailor your marketing push to fit any budget.

It's an unprecedented level of control.

The interface for creating an ad is mostly user-friendly, but the plethora of options can be overwhelming at first. And there are some options that can spend your entire advertising budget overnight, so it's important to learn the ropes before launching a full campaign.

Analytics are available to help authors understand how their ads are being viewed, shared, and clicked, and what the reach is. If you choose to, you can "boost" your ad for an additional fee, and the level of the boost is dependent on how much extra you want to pay.

Having a Facebook page on its own is a helpful tool, and its easy-to-use interface makes it a natural go-to for a limited-time promotion or in-person event. Combined with Facebook ads, many authors are finding it's a game-changer.

ALLi member Mark Dawson offers a comprehensive online course on Facebook advertising for authors, as well as free content to improve your social media marketing. You can sign up at selfpublishingformula.com.

Google Ads

Google Ads is a pay-per-click advertising platform that displays your ad in two ways: alongside Google's search results, and in the Google Display Network, which displays advertisements on a variety of websites.

Anecdotally, Google Ads performs better for nonfiction than fiction.

Google Ads can be profitable, but as with other online advertising platforms, it comes with a learning curve. It's easy to exceed your budget or blow through it in a day if you're not cautious. Learn the ins and outs of advertising on this platform before you create your first ad, start with a small investment and firm limits on daily spending, and monitor your results carefully throughout the life of the ad.

Social Media Broadcasting

Social media offers a means of reaching vast numbers of people, but the immensity of that audience is both its advantage and its liability. While it's possible to promote your book for free or close to it, targeting can be next to impossible, and most advertising is lost in the noise.

Social media promotional services can help with this challenge, and companies that have amassed targeted audiences of followers are uniquely suited to promote your book.

Of the many companies offering these services, one of the most outstanding is BooksGoSocial (BGS). BGS takes a holistic approach to book marketing, offering not only promotion, but detailed and thoughtful recommendations on improving your cover, marketing copy, and more. Best of all, BGS offers an unprecedented money-back guarantee if the results fall short of expectations.

When evaluating social media promotion companies, look to four key factors: reach, targeting, engagement, and metrics.

Reach refers to the number of viewers the service commands. The larger the audience, the higher the number of views your ad is likely to receive. A company that does not disclose these figures should be avoided. But reach—quantity—is only part of the equation. The quality of those accounts is vital, and that's where targeting and engagement come into play.

For your ad to be effective, you need to reach your target audience. Mystery readers may be less likely to click on an ad for science fiction. Horror fans may have no interest in romance novels. The more focused the social media channel is on your genre, or a particular aspect of your book (e.g. discounted ebooks), the better your chances of connecting with readers who will buy it.

One measure of that relevance is engagement—the public's interaction with the social media content. This is particularly important on Facebook, where the number of people who like, share, and comment on a post helps to determine its visibility, or how many people the post will be shown to. Examine the company's social media posts to see how many people are interacting with them. If they are untouched, they are probably unseen as well.

To determine how well your ad is performing, you will need information about the number of views and clicks it receives. Ask your service provider what metrics they provide to help you in this task. If they simply broadcast an ad and provide no information about performance, you have no way of judging whether you are getting your money's worth.

OTHER PROMOTIONAL TOOLS

Contest and Giveaways

Contests and book giveaways can stir up excitement among your readers. Services such as Amazon Giveaway, Goodreads Giveaway, Rafflecopter, and KingSumo provide features to help you organize these events, run them, advertise them, and distribute prizes to winners automatically. Costs for these management services are low, but read the rules to ensure that you're complying with the terms and conditions of the social media platforms you're using.

KDP Select Tools

Amazon's KDP Select is an optional program within KDP that requires authors to sell their ebooks exclusively through Amazon for a 90-day term. In exchange for that exclusivity, the author is granted five days of book promotion, either making the book free, or offering a discount with a countdown timer.

These promotions can be outstanding tools for boosting readership and sales. For maximum impact, pair them with ebook discovery services, as the added exposure amplifies the effect and can even boost your book to the top of its Amazon sales categories.

Press Releases

Press releases are a staple of traditional PR, and an important means of connecting with the media. However, not all press releases are created equal.

The quality of the contacts is paramount when sending out press releases. Many companies that offer this service are essentially blasting one carbon-copy press release after another to an aging mailing list, or worse, simply posting them on a press release website. A shotgun approach will not work here.

An effective press release should be carefully tailored to the recipients, and carefully targeted to those most likely to broadcast news of the book.

Beware of hefty markups on substandard press releases, a hallmark of vanity press marketing packages.

Online Catalogs and Databases

There are countless websites that will display your book and links to retailers. For these platforms to be effective, they must generate sufficient traffic to get your ad in front of your target audience.

In most cases, these sites don't have anywhere near the visitors needed to generate significant sales, even overlooking the fact that your book may be lost among hundreds of others on the site.

If you do consider an online catalogue, ask how much traffic the site receives, and what the demographics of the visitors are. And if this feature is part of a larger marketing package, you may want to disregard it when assessing the overall value of those services.

A similar scheme involves searchable databases, often billed as a way to get your work in the hands of film producers and agents. In this case, the quantity of visitors is less important than the quality. Unfortunately, it can be difficult to assess who is using the site, but you can ask how many clients have had their books optioned through the service. If the answer is vague—"lots!"—be suspicious.

ASSESSING MARKETING AND PROMOTION SERVICES

Self-published authors struggle with marketing and promotion more than any other area. In this and the following section, we highlight some of the pitfalls specific to these services, but to properly assess marketing and promotional services, you must also use the techniques outlined in **Part V, How to Evaluate Self-Publishing Services**

14

PUBLISHING RIGHTS SERVICES

W hile authors tend to focus on book sales as the endgame of the publishing process, each of your books actually represents several sets of rights: ebook, print book (in different formats like hardback and large print) and audiobook are all formats we can do ourselves but when it comes to film, international editions, translations, stage adaptations, merchandising, and more, we need to license rights to other creative companies, services or individuals.

When we talk about authors' "selling rights," what we're referring to is the legal right authors have to grant permission (called a license) to others to exploit some of the author's exclusive rights, such as the right to reproduce the book in print or digital formats, or to translate the work, or to make a film based upon the work.

Under the proper circumstances, these rights can potentially be more valuable than original book rights, so it's important always to understand the licensing terms we're offering.

A discussion of rights could fill a book itself and indeed does! See Orna Ross and Helen Sedwick's *Selective Rights Licensing* for a detailed examination of the issues surrounding rights licensing. For the purposes of this book we'll focus on the concept of **selective**

rights licensing, which is ALLi's recommended policy, and warning signs to look out for when it comes to rights services.

As a self-publisher, if you've followed the advice in this book, all of your rights belong to you. This gives you a tremendous advantage over trade-published authors whose publishers are not exploiting their rights, which is the vast majority of the writers on their books.

Selective Rights Licensing

Selective rights licensing means that rather than granting or assigning all the rights in a title to one publisher, you understand that each right is a separate package, which may be separately licensed in exchange for compensation in the form of a flat fee or royalties (a percentage of sales revenue).

Licenses to publish come in many flavors. They may be exclusive (meaning only the licensee has permission to use the work) or non-exclusive (meaning more than one person may use the work at the same time).

The license limits what can be done with the rights. They may be limited to a particular use (editorial, noncommercial, educational), or format (print, e-book, web), or duration, or territory.

Imagine your book is a shopping center, and you are the landlord. Each empty shop represents a set of rights. One shop might be print books (p-books) in English, another might be audiobooks (a-books) in Spanish, another might be e-books in Mandarin, another might be selling movie tickets and downloads. If your book goes mega and is amenable, your center might even, like Harry Potter, include a theme park.

Since your rent depends entirely on how much each shop sells, you want to rent to companies that have the wherewithal to use those particular rights to make money for you both. In other words, you shouldn't grant rights to the French translation of your book to an English-only publisher that is unlikely to exploit them.

As you learn about, and begin to exploit, the opportunities outlined in this book, keep the landlord analogy in mind.

— SELECTIVE RIGHTS LICENSING BY ORNA ROSS & HELEN SEDWICK

We talk about "selling" our "book" to a publisher, but what we're actually doing when we sign a publishing contract is licensing the right to publish in exchange for an advance, royalties and some publishing services (editorial, design etc).

Selective rights licensing involves making sure that the license you are offering is exclusive to that rights buyer only for publication in a specific format (e.g. print only), within a specific territory (e.g. USA only) and for a specific term (e.g. five years).

Licensing is the term to use, always, in discussions with rights buyers. They may speak of "granting" or "assigning" rights but as indie authors what we want to do is license non-exclusively and selectively, rather than hand across the whole suite of rights to a buyer who has no real plan.

A rights license is *not* a transfer of ownership. "Use it or lose it" is the proper attitude for authors to have toward publishing rights buyers.

Rights buyers will push hard to acquire world ebook rights, audiobook rights and print rights. You will hold hard to limit the format, territory and term. These three are your mantra as a rights seller: format, territory, term.

And your watchword as a selective rights licenser is "non-exclusive". Licensing all rights to one buyer, without due consideration, is an expensive mistake we've seen too many authors make.

Prime Rights and Subsidiary Rights

For an indie author, **subsidiary rights** (sometimes known as "sub rights") are rights outside the big three that we can do ourselves: ebook, print, audio. Until very recently, audio was treated as a sub right but new indie services and digital downloads mean we can now do audio direct—though many of our members choose to (selectively!) license audio rights to an audiobook publisher. The most common sub rights sold by indies are foreign language rights, TV, film, merchandise and games.

As you might imagine, subsidiary rights can be valuable commodities. JK Rowling wisely retained her subsidiary rights for the Harry Potter series, and in 1999 just the film rights for the first four books netted her approximately $2,000,000. Royalties following that initial deal earned millions more.

It is imperative that you understand the value of your copyright, and know which rights you're signing away in a contract and for how long (term) and where (territory).

Be especially wary of contracts that empower the other party to license or sell rights on your behalf. Some exploitative contracts permit this without any input on your part, which means the publisher could sell those valuable subsidiary rights for a pittance. Whenever possible, retain control over the future of your work.

Some self-publishing services (and all trade-publishers) aim to retain rights for a certain period of time in exchange for marketing or promotional services. If you choose to go this path of assisted publishing, it is of the utmost importance for you to completely understand the rights implications.

What, if anything, are they giving you as compensation? In trade-publishing, it should be royalties and ideally an advance. The advance is the measure of the publisher's confidence in a book.

If a service wants you to give them the rights to your material, but is also asking for payment, it's a strong indication that this service is unlikely to be working in your best interests.

A rights licensing marketplace like Pubmatch (see below) can help you connect with buyers, but it's important to be realistic. Rights buyers are heavily saturated, with a great deal of material arriving on their desks every day. Selling rights is always a challenging proposition.

Pubmatch can help to break down some barriers for rights holders and simplify the rights process, but licensing rights is not easy and requires the same sort of dedication as selling your book directly to readers.

When it comes to this stage of the publishing process—and this is not something to even think about until you are already selling sell in English in at least one format—be prepared to invest considerable time and administration in rights management.

PubMatch

PubMatch is a partnership between Publishers Weekly (PW) and the Combined Book Exhibit family of companies, which aims to facilitate rights deals outside of major book fairs like Frankfurt or London. Although PW is based in the US, it has international connections, including a partnership with the London Book Fair and the Alliance of Independent Authors.

The PubMatch website boasts bold infographics explaining how rights break down and which countries offer the most promise.

It offers ways to post your book for publishers and agents to find, as well as various ways to seek out potential business partners accepting titles. The service is geared not only toward writers, but also toward publishers looking for talent and easy ways to connect for rights transactions, as well as toward agents and artistic service providers.

ALLi members get a significant discount with PubMatch and also are included in an ALLi branded portal page on the platform. This enables us to create an ALLi catalogue of members' books that have been uploaded to PubMatch, which we share with rights buyers.

See More: Pubmatch Rights Guide

Copyright Protection

Your work is protected by copyright the moment it's recorded. You may choose to formally register that copyright, which has some advantages, but this is strictly optional.

In the United States, registration with the US Copyright Office is required to bring a lawsuit against someone who has infringed your rights. This is a moot point for most authors, however, as the cost of filing a lawsuit in the US can exceed $100,000, which is beyond the means of the average indie author.

Copyright registration can also be useful for proving ownership of a work. If a retailer such as Amazon challenges your ownership due to perceived similarities to other works, a copyright registration may serve as quick and authoritative evidence of your right to publish.

It costs $35 to register online with the US Copyright Office. The service is available not only to US citizens, but to any resident of a country that holds a copyright treaty with the US, and any author whose work is first published in the US.

Copyright registries exist in other countries, but many of these are private entities with no legal authority. This is especially true in the UK and other countries which lack a governmental copyright registry. Such services are of limited value, but may still serve as formal proof that copyright was established as of the date of filing, in the event of a suit.

Beware the "poor man's copyright," the practice of mailing your work to yourself in a sealed envelope, and relying on the postmark to establish the date of your work's creation. These tactics are easy to fake, and in most jurisdictions have no validity.

PIRACY

Piracy is an ever-present irritant for author-publishers, and no book is beneath the notice of the pirate networks that illegally distribute copyrighted works.

Of course copyright infringers could not operate without readers to download the books but readers are often unaware of the issues involved, or confused about legalities. And, indeed, the legal and technical aspects of book piracy prevention are complex and fast-evolving.

Twenty-five percent of Canadian respondents cited in a 2017 report1 into online copyright infringement had consumed at least one illegally-obtained file in the preceding three months. Almost half of them reported being unsure of what is legal.

Authors attitudes to piracy vary widely. Some ALLi members frequently ask for help removing their copyrighted works from pirate sites. Others are happy to be pirated, believing—like those who chose to give away free books—that piracy is a less significant problem for authors than obscurity. Some even think of piracy as a marketing tool.

It's also worth noting that although there are hundreds of sites claiming to have pirated books, only a few actually do. Most of these sites are actually credit card scams, malware distributors, or other criminal operations. They use scraped listings from Amazon as bait to lure in victims.

Never click on a link in a pirate site to verify whether it legitimately has a copy of your book. Doing so can expose you to malware or compromise your personal information.

Takedown Notices

When a copyright owner discovers that a web-hosting company is housing unlawful material, a DMCA notice in writing to the web-hosting company is the method used to demand takedown.

Although technically a US law, the existence of the Digital Millennium Copyright Act (1998) has allowed similar action to be taken in all territories.

However, individual DMCA takedown notices are often ineffective. It's "whack-a-mole." For example, one of the most persistent ebook pirate sites, with over 120,000 take-down notices against it, has been taken down multiple times, only to emerge again under a different .com, .net or .org domain name. Threats from lawyers, domain hosts and the police have done nothing to stop it.

On the other hand, some sites are compliant once informed of infringement.

The UK Publishers Association runs a Copyright Infringement Portal (CIP), an independent online system to help combat digital piracy. It identifies infringing links and streamlines the takedown notice creation process.

If you've found your books being shared online without your permission the PA's CIP could help you get them removed from the web. ALLi members have a special arrangement, with discounted access to CIP.com at various levels.

Find out more about CIP at: ALLiMembers.org/piracy

ALLi's *Copyright Bill of Rights* gives the background to indie author approaches to piracy and plagiarism and the fundamental importance of copyright.

Literary Agencies

While many authors like to have an agent on their side, we should remember that the purpose of an agent is to make you more money than you can make for yourself. If your agent hasn't sold any rights for you, or hasn't provided significant publicity opportunities, then you may be on their books, but you don't really have an agent.

The response of literary agents to self-publishing varies widely. Some are not interested at all, seeing trade publishing as the arena in which they make money for themselves and authors. For others—and it must be said the less successful agencies—self-publishing is providing a way for them to stay afloat in a changing publishing environment.

What has come to be called "agent assisted self-publishing" can take many different forms. At one end of the scale, it means an agency encouraging an author to upload unsaleable manuscripts or out-of-print backlist books and showing them how, without taking any payment. The reasoning is that self-published titles can give a revenue boost to the author's trade-published titles, which the agency does represent. And that every improvement to an author's platform is worthwhile.

At the other end are unscrupulous agents actively seeking unpublished writers to "assist", calling for the author to finance production and marketing, while the file gets uploaded in the agent's name and account. For the work of managing the digital dashboard the agent receives 15 percent of income for the life of the book.

Some authors believe, or are being persuaded, that choosing this route and paying that 15 percent will smooth a pathway to trade-publication.

Few of these deals are good for authors, who lose their ability to directly manage their books indefinitely. We advise that authors do the same due diligence as with any self-publishing service. Take time to understand what you are giving up in order to be agent-assisted, and what you stand to gain.

The key considerations when it comes to AASP are as follows:

1. Who holds the rights and for how long? Always ask about reversion, and beware of early termination fees in contracts.

2. What is the commission split? With Kobo, Apple iBooks, and some KDP territories, the maximum author commission is 70 percent. No digital publisher or literary agency can get you more than that. If you question closely, you may find they are using the same platforms and giving you less, a percentage of their receipts, and sometimes minus their costs. So what are they offering in return for this lesser commission?

3. What marketing support is provided? Marketing is the only commercial reason you may want to go with an agency or digital publisher. It is crucial to ask what marketing they'll be doing that you can't do for yourself. If it's Facebook ads, who's in charge of that? What about reviews? Blog tours? Is their proposed support ongoing, as digital marketing needs to be? If it's showing you how to manage social media, that's not marketing, that's training. Consider whether you really want to sign away your rights in return or if you'd rather invest in a short-term course and learn to do it yourself?

ALLi Members: for more on publishing rights, including a free download of our guidebook by ALLi Director Orna Ross and self-publishing legal expert, Helen Sedwick; advice on how to manage and negotiate rights see AlliMembers.org/rights.

PART III

ASSISTED SELF-PUBLISHING

15

PACKAGED SERVICES

W hile there are many exceptional service providers, it is in this arena of bundled services that we see some of the most egregious fraud and exploitative behavior. Hidden, inflated pricing is everywhere. If your service provider does not offer an itemized breakdown of prices, be suspicious: they may be hiding something from you.

It's rare to find a company that specializes in every aspect of book production, especially one with a limited staff and resources. Thus, you may find that a self-publishing package provides excellent editing and formatting, but lackluster cover design. Or they may provide outstanding design, but ineffective and costly marketing.

You are statistically less likely to receive high quality from a company that provides a wide range of services than one that focuses exclusively on one service. Examine the company's work for each service you plan to purchase, and whenever possible, use companies that allow you to opt out of specific services so that you can choose the best available providers.

Beginner authors sometimes sign up for self-publishing packages that are presented to them as "being published". Publishers don't ask for payment. If you are contributing to the costs, you are working with a self-publishing service.

UNNECESSARY ADD-ONS

The value-added service—a bonus or add-on service that complements a primary purchase—is a sales tactic we see every day:

"Your hotel stay includes free Wi-Fi and a continental breakfast."

"If you upgrade to the Deluxe package, the five-year extended warranty is included automatically."

"Would you like fries with that for just a dollar more?"

At their best, these offerings provide a welcome bargain. But at their worst, they can be used to deceive and defraud consumers.

Car dealerships are notorious for inflating the price of a car with high-profit, low-value extras. They'll offer floor mats, car alarms, upgraded upholstery, extended dealer warranties, clear coat, rust-proofing (the car isn't rustproof already?), tinted windows, vehicle ID number etching, cruise control, GPS, the "deluxe" stereo system... and suddenly, that $30,000 retail price has nearly doubled.

These costs are often bundled into a package that makes it hard to determine the value of the individual components. What's presented as a convenience may actually be predatory pricing hidden under a mountain of fluff. To determine if you're getting a good deal on a package, you'll need to separate that fluff from the services of real value.

The following services are commonly used to pad self-publishing packages, either as an add-on service or as a bundled feature with questionable value to the author.

Please note that these services are not inherently bad. However, they deserve extra scrutiny when their price tag is concealed among other bundled services.

Copyright Registration and LCCN

Copyright registrations in the US and other jurisdictions are simple and inexpensive. In the US, where copyright registration is a prerequisite for filing suit against infringing parties, the process can be completed online in about five minutes, at a cost of $35.

Similarly, obtaining a Library of Congress Control Number (LCCN) is as simple as opening a free account and submitting your book's information. There is no cost, and you'll receive your LCCN within a few days.

There is no credible reason for an author to pay $100 or more for these simple, inexpensive procedures.

Press Releases

To be successful, a press release must have an engaging headline, a unique angle, and informative, well-crafted content. It should be part of an intelligent marketing strategy, and it must be targeted to the right journalists at the right venues. There is an art to writing effective press releases.

With that in mind, consider these press release headlines churned out by one provider as part of its publishing package:

A Breathtaking Thriller that Delves into the Mayhem and Enigma of Deceit and Evil

A Breathtaking Thriller that Delves into the Mayhem and Enigma of Deceit and Love

A Breathtaking Thriller That Delves Into the Mayhem and Enigma of Deceit and Faith

A Breathtaking Thriller that Delves into the Mayhem and Enigma of Deceit and Murder

A Breathtaking Thriller that Delves into the Mayhem and Enigma of War and Government

---

A fill-in-the-blanks approach like this ensures that your press release will be ignored. (To add insult to injury, more than a third of the text of each press release above was dedicated to promoting the publishing service rather than the book.)

If you choose to purchase a press release as part of a package, be sure the provider is qualified to handle your publicity. Investigate its past work, and use Google search on titles it represents to see if the press releases were actually picked up by media outlets. Verify that the press releases are unique and tailored to the individual work.

If the provider doesn't have a solid PR track record, then its press release may be a breathtaking waste of money that delves into the mayhem of deceit and exploitation.

Inclusion in Catalogues

Catalogues from obscure publishers flood the market today. When mass-mailed to retailers, libraries, or journalists, these unsolicited catalogues are destined for the trash heap.

Don't waste good money on dumpster lining.

Another red flag is expensive display advertising in magazines like *Kirkus* and *Publisher's Weekly*. Readers do not read these magazines, and those who do—librarians and book industry people—generally make buying decisions based on the editorial, not the ads. Be very wary of such packages unless you have a clear underlying strategy that includes them.

Publicity and PR Campaigns

An effective PR campaign is carefully targeted and multifaceted. Unfortunately, some assisted self-publishing services take a quantity-over-quality approach, blindly spewing out the aforementioned press releases and catalogues to every agent, publisher, or media outlet they can find. Professionals despise this kind of shotgun approach and tend to delete them on sight. And obviously, those communications do no good if they go directly into a wastebasket or spam folder.

Before considering a paid publicity campaign—and they're not cheap—find out exactly what you're paying for. How, exactly, will it promote your brand?

Look for independent evidence of the provider's successful campaigns. Are clients being featured on radio and TV segments? Are they being covered by journalists? Or is there no trace of those authors outside of the provider's website?

If there's scant evidence that these campaigns are working, you're not likely to be the exception to that rule.

Complimentary Copies

Complimentary copies of your book are nice to have, but weigh their value against the price you're paying for the whole package.

In the continental US, ten copies of a 240-page book will cost approximately $48 on KDP. That's a tiny percentage of the cost of some assisted publishing packages, so keep the relative benefit of this perk in perspective. In these instances, the term "complimentary" just means the cost of the books has been factored into the price of the package already.

Retailer Previews

Google Preview, Amazon's Look Inside the Book feature, and other retailer previews are free benefits available to any author publishing on those platforms. Needless to say, if service providers try to take credit for that feature as a value-added service they are providing, they are not being entirely honest.

Retailer previews are standard features provided free of charge, so scratch this one off any list of supposed benefits a service provider offers.

Closed Awards and Recognition Programs

These are a common ploy among the larger vanity press schemes. By purchasing a package, you become eligible for an award or "recognition program." It's essentially a pay-to-play contest that's only open to the small subset of authors who have coughed up several hundred dollars to that vendor. The award itself carries little significance for the average reader, and so the contest provides more benefit to the seller than to the author.

Accounting

Proper accounting is not a feature; it's a requirement for any reputable service. If a provider lists accounting as an added benefit, cast a skeptical eye on that claim. If it charges you a fee to access an accounting dashboard, turn and walk away.

Proofs

Does the provider expect you to accept its work without your review or approval? Not if it's a reputable company. Digital previews and proof copies are a requirement for any service that prepares your books, not a benefit that sets it apart.

Social Media Promotion

Social media can be an excellent channel for promotion, but there's more to it than simply churning out ads. Be wary of service providers who promise social media promotion but who lack the audience and engagement to make it work.

For example, a provider claims it will increase your exposure by promoting your book to its Facebook fans. On inspection, the Facebook page has just under 1,000 fans after three years of operation — an unimpressive number for a provider that offers social media services. Worse, each post is an advertisement that has at most one or two likes.

If the provider can't successfully promote its own products and services, how will it promote yours? If it can't hold the interest of people who have explicitly liked its page, how will it gain the attention of an audience that doesn't know you?

Author Page on the Service Provider's Website

Unless the provider attracts massive traffic, a page on its website—even one that's prominently featured—is not a valuable offering. Beware of claims of improved exposure without solid numbers to back them up.

One word of warning about metrics: don't be misled by the term "hits" when a provider describes its web traffic. A "hit" is simply a request for one element on a page: an image, a video, a script file, a font, etc. A single visit to one page may generate dozens of hits. Providers that describe their web traffic in terms of hits may be trying to deceive you, or they may be genuinely unaware of the uselessness of that metric.

Either one is cause for concern.

Reviews

Due to widespread author dissatisfaction, high cost, and a lack of tangible results, editorial reviews in general are considered to be a poor investment, even when purchased from a respected source such as Kirkus. When purchased from a provider that carries no name recognition among readers, they are no more credible than your Aunt Becky's glowing praise.

If you do opt to purchase an editorial review, either à la carte or as part of a package, be sure the reviewer has credibility and name recognition. If the provider is reselling a review from a third-party service like Kirkus, comparison shop to see if it is gouging with huge markups. Unscrupulous providers often resell reviews at astronomical markups, sometimes as much as 700% over Kirkus's already steep pricing.

ASSESSING FEES

Working with a dedicated provider of a single service is a clear proposition: you pay x, you receive y. But in a package of services, fees may not be itemized, and so poor value and inflated prices can easily be concealed amid a lengthy list of services.

Perform your own cost breakdown by itemizing each service included in the package. If it's unclear what services are being provided—a lack of transparency and clarity that should be considered a red flag—ask the service provider to explain in detail what you're getting for your money.

Now, with a detailed list of services, you can comparison shop. Look for companies that specialize in each service, and try to select services that match your candidate's offerings as closely as possible. Gather fees from a variety of services to determine the prevailing range of prices. Use only reputable, vetted services for this, as you don't want to judge the value of a service against the worst examples in the field.

Finally, with a range of prices for these services in hand, you can determine the average cost for each. Add them up, and compare the total to your candidate's quoted price.

This method offers only a rough assessment. It's sometimes hard to find services that are a fair equivalence, and there are countless hard-to-quantify factors that can affect the price of a service—quality, experience, and so on. But in the absence of other indicators, this method can give you a quick back-of-the-envelope reckoning to guide your decision.

16

VANITY PRESSES

LLi's definition of a vanity press is one that engages in misleading or, in the worst cases, outright deceptive practices, with the intention not of bringing books to readers but of extracting as much money as possible from the authors.

They sell a dream, presenting expensive services in a manner that exploits new authors' hopes for their work. They exaggerate and blur lines, so that naive authors believe they have been published, when all that has happened is their book has been printed, often at greater cost than they would have paid their local printer.

Like bad used-car sales staff, these publishers fail to point to the scratches on the body (the flaws in the book) or the cracked chassis (the lack of real distribution or marketing services in their offering).

We regularly hear of naive or uninformed authors who are left with a basement, attic, or garage full of books they have been pressured into buying and which they have no hope of selling. Such operations, some charging five-digit fees, proliferate on the internet and have the highest number of self-published titles each year.

ALLi knows of services that have used false addresses in affluent areas to reel in the unwary author; services where the personnel use false names and aliases; services that take a fee and an exclusivity license, not allowing the author to publish elsewhere; services that require the author to purchase a substantial number of copies of the book; and a great many services that trade on misleading promises and vague language.

The worst of these operators will do anything to get the author to pay for services, and often shoddy services at that. Work that hasn't been read is lauded; the "gatekeeping" of trade-publishers is demonized; a veil of complexity is thrown over the publishing process; and sales reps bombard the prospective customer with emails and phone calls that urge them to do the right thing by their book.

These exploitative services are legion. A Google search for "self-publishing services" will return advertisements for many of the worst operators, all promising success.

Assaulted with omnipresent, aggressive marketing and high-pressure sales, any novice author starts their self-publishing journey in peril.

Author Solutions

When it comes to author services, one company tends to get particular attention due to its size, global reach, and the unfortunate support of well-known publishing brand names. Author Solutions (ASI) is the umbrella name for a network of controversial companies distrusted by authors in the know.

Tragically, despite innumerable complaints, multiple class-action lawsuits, and constant rebuke by author watchdogs, ASI is often the first port of call for uninformed writers seeking a publishing service. Novice authors are lured in by ASI's aggressive marketing and omnipresent advertisements. Because they do not research the company's background, many prove to be easy prey.

Even those aware of ASI's reputation need to be vigilant: There is no publishing house called "Author Solutions." It trades under a variety of imprints, including Xlibris, Archway, LifeRich, iUniverse, Trafford, Abbott Press, Balboa, AuthorHouse US & UK, Partridge,

Palibrio (ASI's Spanish language imprint), and WestBow, to name a few.

Some of these imprints are more author-centric than others, but none follow what ALLi promotes as best practices or fully abides by our Code of Standards. In our opinion, most fall at the first clause: "We follow through on all promised services and fully honor all advertisements and publication agreement terms. We never spam, oversell, or harass authors to buy our services or sell a dream to the uninitiated."

We have tried to discuss this with ASI but with unsatisfactory responses. As well as ALLi, author activists like Nate Hoffelder, David Gaughran, Jim Giammatteo, Mick Rooney, Victoria Strauss, and many others have expressed concern over ASI's treatment of authors. In the US, where the parent company is located, class-action lawsuits have been filed against ASI and its former parent company, Penguin Random House.

The authors in one of these suits alleged breach of contract, unjust enrichment and various violations of the California Business and Professional Code, and of New York General Business Law. Ultimately, Penguin Random House was dismissed from the case, along with some—but not all—of the claims against ASI. The case was settled in August 2015 and discontinued, but not before revealing that only one-third of ASI's revenue comes from selling books to readers. Two-thirds of its revenue comes from selling services to authors. The terms of the settlement were not released.

Avoiding Vanity Presses

As venerable trade-publishers, long-established agents, and new digital-only imprints all get involved in providing self-publishing services, intent has become the core criterion by which we judge services.

ALLi urges authors to be vigilant and to put services under a microscope before parting with money. Compare what you're getting with offerings from providers that get a good rating in this guide, like KDP, Kobo, PublishDrive, StreetLib, Draft2Digital, and IngramSpark.

Talk to other authors, and don't be lured by false or vague half-promises. Under such scrutiny, more often than not, the price tag for a publishing package quickly goes from being good value to looking very extortionate indeed.

17

HYBRID PRESSES

In a traditional publishing relationship, the publisher is responsible for the development and production of a book, and in return for these services retains a large share of the sale price of every book. The publisher never takes money from the author, and profit is dependent wholly on the success of the book.

In an assisted self-publishing relationship, the author pays for specific services. The service provider makes their money primarily from the sale of services, and it's the author who bears responsibility for the success of the book.

Hybrid publishing attempts to straddle the line between these two models, offering a traditional publishing framework including curation and physical bookstore distribution, but charging the author to offset the cost of production.

Although there are ethical and reputable hybrid publishers, there are many more substandard services that have turned to hybrid publishing, sometimes as a means of camouflaging exploitative vanity press operations. The term can give a veneer to a business model that's actually geared toward extracting as much money as possible from the author.

JOHN DOPPLER & ALLIANCE OF INDEPENDENT AUTHORS

The model is fraught with danger for a couple of key underlying reasons.

Burden of Risk

- Traditional publishers earn their money from the sales of books. If the book does not succeed, the publisher does not profit. The central maxim of publishing is that income should flow from publisher to author but in a hybrid publishing arrangement, the publisher collects payment from the author upfront. If the book fails to sell, the hybrid publisher has already been paid. It's the author who is out of pocket.
- Hybrid publishing shifts the burden of risk to the author. For this model to be beneficial to the author, that burden of risk requires compensation in the form of significantly improved royalties. Regardless of the compensation, it is always the author who potentially stands to lose money and the publisher who gains in this relationship.

Low Incentive to Promote

- Because the hybrid publisher receives money in advance, any investment in promotion and marketing comes out of its profits. With money already in hand, there is an inherently lower incentive for hybrid publishers to invest those funds in the promotion of the author's books.

Not all hybrid publishers are exploitative, but authors must take great care to weed out those that are. ALLi advises extreme caution when considering this kind of publishing arrangement.

Here is a partial list of what I look for when evaluating hybrids for the Alliance of Independent Authors:

1. The company acts in the full capacity of a traditional publisher, providing multi-level editing, cover design, publishing and distribution, marketing, sales, and accounting services.

2. The publisher has a well-established track record of professional conduct, high quality, and successful marketing as either a traditional publisher, or as a fee-for-service provider.

3. Submissions are curated; the publisher declines submissions which they cannot successfully market or which do not fit the company's focus.

4. The publisher offers compensation commensurate with the burden of risk shouldered by the author. At the absolute minimum, a 50% share of the net (from distributors/retailers) or its equivalent is appropriate.

5. The publisher sells books to readers, not the author. Mandatory purchases of books are unacceptable, whether explicitly or as a hidden charge in the guise of "bonus author copies".

6. The publisher has a clearly articulated strategy for marketing and promoting its titles.

7. The publisher offers services and advantages which are not generally available from fee-for-service providers, such as superior distribution or media contacts.

8. Rights and licenses granted by the author are fully leveraged by the publisher, with appropriate compensation. Unused rights automatically revert to the author within a set period of time.

9. Contract terms are unambiguous, protect the author as well as the publisher, expire within a reasonable time, and define the circumstances under which the contract may be terminated.

10. The publisher profits from the sale of the books, not author fees. Fees charged to the author are specifically to offset publication costs, with proper accounting.

ALLi's other criteria also apply, such as not commingling paid services with traditional publishing models, not having ties to vanity presses or criminal schemes, and so on. We have few approved Partner Members who offer themselves as hybrid publishers.

PART IV

ALLI'S SERVICE RATINGS

THE RATINGS

18

ABOUT ALLI'S SERVICE RATINGS

The primary purpose of the ALLi Service Ratings is to separate reputable self-publishing services from the rogue operators who over-promise, overcharge, under-deliver, or in any way exploit authors.

ALLi is willing to work with any service that wants to improve its offerings and bring them in line with our recommendations for current best practice for author services.

Contact the Watchdog Desk at any time if you would like to inform us about a service or discuss a rating.

Service providers are listed in alphabetical order for easy lookup, and are assigned one of five possible ratings:

PARTNER MEMBER
Services that have been carefully vetted and which align with ALLi's Code of Standards.

RECOMMENDED
Services that behave ethically and professionally, with pricing and value in line with industry norms.

MIXED
Services that behave ethically and professionally, but fall short of ALLi's Code of Standards in one or more areas.

CAUTION
Services that do not align with one or more aspects of the ALLi Code of Standards. These services should be avoided.

WATCHDOG ADVISORY
Services that have given rise to consistent complaints, and which may have been subject to legal action.

The ratings below are the opinions of the ALLi Watchdog Desk, based on careful appraisals of pricing and value, quality of service, contract rights, transparency, accountability, and customer satisfaction. To avoid driving traffic to substandard services, we do not generally give a website address for those rated as CAUTION or WATCHDOG ADVISORY.

Please note that while we update this book regularly, ratings can change overnight and ALLi's ratings are updated frequently online. For the most current information, see: SelfPublishingAdvice.org/ratings.

Contact the Watchdog Desk at any time if you would like to suggest a service for evaluation or share your experiences with a service provider.

You can reach me at: john@allianceindependentauthors.org

1106 Design (Michele DeFilippo)
1106design.com
<small>RECOMMENDED PARTNER MEMBER</small>
Excellent.

Abbott Press
<small>WATCHDOG ADVISORY</small>
An Author Solutions vanity press imprint.

Eleanor Abraham
eleanorabraham.com
<small>RECOMMENDED PARTNER MEMBER</small>
Excellent.

Adirondack Editing
adirondackediting.com
<small>RECOMMENDED PARTNER MEMBER</small>
Excellent.

Aegitas
<small>CAUTION</small>

AIA Editing and Publishing
aiapublishing.com
<small>RECOMMENDED PARTNER MEMBER</small>
Excellent.

Alison's Editing Service
alisonjack-editor.co.uk
<small>RECOMMENDED PARTNER MEMBER</small>
Excellent.

Alliant Press
WATCHDOG ADVISORY
A partnership between Alliant University and Author Solutions. Be
wary of any services offered.

Amazon (KDP)
kdp.amazon.com
RECOMMENDED PARTNER MEMBER
Excellent.

America Star Books
WATCHDOG ADVISORY
Formerly PublishAmerica, a vanity press with a staggering number of
complaints.

Amolibros
amolibros-selfpublishing.co.uk
MIXED

Anthemion Software
anthemion.co.uk
RECOMMENDED PARTNER MEMBER
Excellent.

Apple (iBooks)
apple.com/itunes/working-itunes/sell-content/books/book-faq.html
RECOMMENDED

Archway Publishing
WATCHDOG ADVISORY
Simon & Schuster imprint outsourced to vanity press Author
Solutions.

Areo Books
areobooks.com
RECOMMENDED

AtlasBooks
CAUTION
A division of Bookmasters.

Austin Macauley
WATCHDOG ADVISORY

Author's Republic
authorsrepublic.com
RECOMMENDED PARTNER MEMBER
Excellent.

Author-ity Authors (Dixie Maria Carlton)
authorityauthors.com.au
RECOMMENDED PARTNER MEMBER
Excellent.

Author Accelerator
authoraccelerator.com
RECOMMENDED PARTNER MEMBER
Excellent.

Author Connections
authorconnections.com
RECOMMENDED PARTNER MEMBER
Excellent.

Author Design Studio
authordesignstudio.com
RECOMMENDED PARTNER MEMBER
Excellent.

AuthorHouse
WATCHDOG ADVISORY
An Author Solutions vanity press imprint.

AuthorHouse UK
WATCHDOG ADVISORY
An Author Solutions vanity press imprint.

Authoright
CAUTION

Author Learning Center
CAUTION
Owned by Author Solutions; be extremely wary of any paid services.

Author Marketing Club
authormarketingclub.com
RECOMMENDED

Author Marketing Experts
amarketingexpert.com
RECOMMENDED PARTNER MEMBER
Excellent.

The Author Site
theauthorsite.com
RECOMMENDED PARTNER MEMBER
Excellent.

Author Solutions
WATCHDOG ADVISORY
Author Solutions is the parent corporation of many vanity press imprints, and has been the subject of multiple class-action lawsuits in the US.

Autocrit
autocrit.com
RECOMMENDED

Helen Baggott
helenbaggott.co.uk
RECOMMENDED PARTNER MEMBER
Excellent.

Bakerview Consulting
bakerviewconsulting.com
RECOMMENDED

Balboa Press
WATCHDOG ADVISORY
Hay House imprint outsourced to vanity press Author Solutions.

Balboa Press UK
WATCHDOG ADVISORY
Hay House imprint outsourced to vanity press Author Solutions.

BAM! Publish (Books-A-Million)
booksamillion.com
MIXED

Barbara Bauer Literary Agency
WATCHDOG ADVISORY

Bargain Booksy (Written Word Media)
bargainbooksy.com
RECOMMENDED PARTNER MEMBER
Excellent.

BB EBooks
bbebooksthailand.com
RECOMMENDED PARTNER MEMBER
Excellent.

Jessica Bell
jessicabellauthor.com/book-cover-design-services.html
RECOMMENDED

Berge Design
bergedesign.com
RECOMMENDED PARTNER MEMBER
Excellent.

BetaBooks
BetaBooks.co
RECOMMENDED

Better Scribe
betterscribe.com
RECOMMENDED PARTNER MEMBER
Excellent.

Katie Birks Branding & Design
katiebirks.co.uk
RECOMMENDED PARTNER MEMBER
Excellent.

Black Rose Writing
CAUTION
A history of problematic contract terms, required purchases of authors' books, and various vanity press tactics make this publisher a no-go.

Blank Slate Communications

blankslatecommunications.com/about-us.html

RECOMMENDED PARTNER MEMBER

Excellent.

Blasty

CAUTION

Customer service failures and billing irregularities led to a downgrade of Blasty's rating.

Blissetts

blissetts.com

RECOMMENDED PARTNER MEMBER

Excellent.

Bluebird Consulting

bluebird-consulting.com

RECOMMENDED

BlueInk Review

blueinkreview.com

RECOMMENDED PARTNER MEMBER

Excellent.

Bluewave Publishing

bluewavepublishing.co.uk

RECOMMENDED

Blurb

blurb.com

RECOMMENDED

Blurb offers a number of hard-to-find print formats.

BookBaby
bookbaby.com
RECOMMENDED PARTNER MEMBER
Excellent.

BookBlast
bookblast.com
RECOMMENDED
Please note that BookBlast, a company with a proven track record, is not the same as BookBlastPro, a questionable imitator listed below.

BookBlastPro
WATCHDOG ADVISORY
Please note that BookBlast, a RECOMMENDED company with a proven track record, is unrelated to BookBlastPro.

BookBub
bookbub.com
RECOMMENDED

Book Country
CAUTION
Book Country is owned by Author Solutions; while the community itself is innocuous, be extremely wary of any paid services.

Book Cover Cafe
bookcovercafe.com
RECOMMENDED PARTNER MEMBER
Excellent.

Book Cover Express
bookcoverexpress.com
RECOMMENDED PARTNER MEMBER
Excellent.

Book Create Service

bookcreateservice.com

RECOMMENDED PARTNER MEMBER

Excellent.

The Book Designer (Joel Friedlander)

thebookdesigner.com

RECOMMENDED PARTNER MEMBER

Excellent.

BookFunnel

bookfunnel.com

RECOMMENDED

BookGarage

bookgarage.com

RECOMMENDED PARTNER MEMBER

Excellent.

Book Industry Communication (BIC)

bic.org.uk

RECOMMENDED

BookLocker

booklocker.com

RECOMMENDED

Bookmasters

CAUTION

Also operates as AtlasBooks.

Book Nanny

booknannyfictioneditor.com

RECOMMENDED

Bookouture
bookouture.com
RECOMMENDED

Bookprinting.com
CAUTION

BookPublishing.com (Jenkins Group)
CAUTION

Book Reality
bookreality.com
RECOMMENDED

Bookrix
bookrix.com
CAUTION
Troubling contract terms and spammy marketing.

BookRunes
bookrunes.com/submit-book
RECOMMENDED

Books Butterfly
booksbutterfly.com
CAUTION
Numerous complaints place this service on our CAUTION list.

BooksGoSocial
booksgosocial.com
RECOMMENDED PARTNER MEMBER
Excellent.

The Books Machine
thebooksmachine.com
MIXED
Spammy marketing and poor ROI preclude a RECOMMENDED rating on this otherwise ethical service.

BooksOnline.directory
WATCHDOG ADVISORY
Also operates ArtistsGallery.directory and CreativeDesignersWriters.com.

BooksOnline.best
WATCHDOG ADVISORY
Another incarnation of Crystalline Noble. This site is currently flagged by Norton as a potential security risk (and rightfully so). ALLi recommends that authors avoid creating an account on this site or providing them with personal or financial information.

Booktango
WATCHDOG ADVISORY
An Author Solutions vanity press imprint.

Bookupy
CAUTION

BookVenture
bookventure.com
CAUTION
Beyond the outrageous pricing, spammy and unprofessional marketing coupled with overblown claims of an affiliation with Ingram warrant a strong CAUTION rating.

Bowker
myidentifiers.com
MIXED
Although Bowker is a trustworthy source for ISBN registrations (and the only authorized registrar in the US), its ancillary and self-publishing services are a poor value.

Breezeway Books
CAUTION
Formerly Llumina Press.

Averill Buchanan
averillbuchanan.com
RECOMMENDED PARTNER MEMBER
Excellent.

Buzbooks.com
buzbooks.com
RECOMMENDED PARTNER MEMBER
Excellent.

Caliburn Press
CAUTION

Chanticleer Book Reviews
chantireviews.com
RECOMMENDED PARTNER MEMBER
Excellent.

Choosy Bookworm
CAUTION

Karen Cioffi-Ventrice
karencioffiwritingforchildren.com
RECOMMENDED PARTNER MEMBER
Excellent.

Clays
clays.co.uk
RECOMMENDED PARTNER MEMBER
Excellent.

Clink Street Publishing
CAUTION
The "publishing" arm of Authoright.

Clio Editing Service
clioediting.com
RECOMMENDED PARTNER MEMBER
Excellent.

Coinlea Services
coinlea.co.uk
RECOMMENDED PARTNER MEMBER
Excellent.

Completely Novel
completelynovel.com
RECOMMENDED PARTNER MEMBER
Excellent.

Conscious Care Publishing
CAUTION

Cre8urbrand (Jason Conway)
cre8urbrand.co.uk
RECOMMENDED

CreateThinkDo
createthinkdo.com
RECOMMENDED PARTNER MEMBER
Excellent.

CreativeDesignersWriters.com
WATCHDOG ADVISORY
Also operates ArtistsGallery.directory and BooksOnline.directory.

The Creative Penn (Joanna Penn)
thecreativepenn.com
RECOMMENDED PARTNER MEMBER
Excellent.

Creativia
creativia.org
CAUTION

Crystalline Noble
WATCHDOG ADVISORY
Also operates BooksOnline.directory, ArtistsGallery.directory, and
CreativeDesignersWriters.com. Avoid this network of questionable
sites.

Daisy Editorial
daisyeditorial.co.uk
RECOMMENDED PARTNER MEMBER
Excellent.

Damonza.com
damonza.com
RECOMMENDED PARTNER MEMBER
Excellent.

Daniel Goldsmith Associates
danielgoldsmith.co.uk
RECOMMENDED

DartFrog Books
dartfrogbooks.com
RECOMMENDED PARTNER MEMBER
Excellent.

Mark Dawson (Self Publishing Formula)
selfpublishingformula.com
RECOMMENDED PARTNER MEMBER
Excellent.

DCP
CAUTION
Operates msbuyer.com, a manuscript purchasing operation. Actual company name and location are unknown, but operates under the alias "DCP."

Design for Writers
designforwriters.com
RECOMMENDED PARTNER MEMBER
Excellent.

Dick Margulis Creative Services
dmargulis.com
RECOMMENDED

Dissect Designs (Tim Barber)
dissectdesigns.com
RECOMMENDED PARTNER MEMBER
Excellent.

Dog Ear Publishing
WATCHDOG ADVISORY
Numerous complaints alleging failure to pay royalties, and refusal to communicate with authors.

Dorrance Publishing
CAUTION

Libby Doyle (Fairhill Publishing LLC)
libbydoyle.com/editing-services.html
RECOMMENDED PARTNER MEMBER
Excellent.

Draft2Digital
draft2digital.com
RECOMMENDED PARTNER MEMBER
Excellent.

Katharine D'Souza
katharinedsouza.co.uk
RECOMMENDED PARTNER MEMBER
Excellent.

eBook Dynasty
ebookdynasty.net
RECOMMENDED PARTNER MEMBER
Excellent.

Ebook Launch
ebooklaunch.com
RECOMMENDED PARTNER MEMBER
Excellent.

eBook Partnership
ebookpartnership.com
RECOMMENDED

eBooksAreForever
ebooksareforever.com
RECOMMENDED

Ebooks Cover Design
ebookscoversdesign.com
RECOMMENDED

Editorial.ie
editorial.ie
RECOMMENDED PARTNER MEMBER
Excellent.

Elly Donovan PR
ellydonovan.co.uk
RECOMMENDED PARTNER MEMBER
Excellent.

FastPencil
CAUTION

FCM Publishing
fcmpublishing.co.uk
RECOMMENDED PARTNER MEMBER
Excellent.

FicFun
CAUTION
Submissions are subject to a rights grab for the life of the copyright.

Fiction Feedback
fictionfeedback.co.uk
RECOMMENDED PARTNER MEMBER
Excellent.

FindPublishingHelp.com
CAUTION
Lead generator for problematic vanity presses. Aggressive marketing.

Fingerpress Ltd
fingerpress.com
RECOMMENDED PARTNER MEMBER
Excellent.

First Edition Design Publishing
CAUTION

Five Rainbows (Lisa A. Shiel)
fiverainbows.com
RECOMMENDED
An excellent service provider offering PCIP data and MARC records.

Formatting Experts
formattingexperts.com
RECOMMENDED PARTNER MEMBER
Excellent.

FreeBooksy (Written Word Media)
freebooksy.com
RECOMMENDED PARTNER MEMBER
Excellent.

Fulton Books
CAUTION

Fussy Librarian
thefussylibrarian.com
RECOMMENDED

GABAL Global Editions
WATCHDOG ADVISORY
GABAL imprint outsourced to Author Solutions.

Gatekeeper Press
gatekeeperpress.com
RECOMMENDED

Get Published! LLC
WATCHDOG ADVISORY
This parent company of Author Solutions does not offer publishing services directly.

GetPublishingHelp.com
WATCHDOG ADVISORY
An anonymous lead-gathering website run by New Century Publishing, a vanity publisher that was the target of a lawsuit by the Indiana State Attorney General following numerous consumer complaints.

Girl Friday Productions
girlfridayproductions.com
RECOMMENDED PARTNER MEMBER
Excellent.

Grammarly
grammarly.com
RECOMMENDED

Green Ivy Publishing
CAUTION
Reported out of business.

Guaranteed Author (Leigh St. John)
CAUTION

Gunboss Books
gunboss.com
RECOMMENDED PARTNER MEMBER
Excellent.

Happy Self Publishing
happyselfpublishing.com
RECOMMENDED

Heddon Publishing
heddonpublishing.com
RECOMMENDED PARTNER MEMBER
Excellent.

Hellgate Press
CAUTION
Hellgate's concealed subsidy publishing program is cause for concern.

Hemingway Editor
hemingwayapp.com
RECOMMENDED

Hillcrest Media Group / Hillcrest Publishing Group
CAUTION

Hobthross Ltd
hobthross.com/index.html
RECOMMENDED PARTNER MEMBER
Excellent.

Hot Pink Publishing (Carla Wynn Hall)
CAUTION

iBooks (Apple)
apple.com/itunes/working-itunes/sell-content/books/book-faq.html
RECOMMENDED

Independent Author Network
independentauthornetwork.com
RECOMMENDED PARTNER MEMBER
Excellent.

Independent Ink
independentink.com.au
RECOMMENDED PARTNER MEMBER
Excellent.

Indie Authors World
indieauthorsworld.com
RECOMMENDED PARTNER MEMBER
Excellent.

IndieBookLauncher
indiebooklauncher.com
RECOMMENDED PARTNER MEMBER
Excellent.

Indie Writer Support
WATCHDOG ADVISORY
Also operates ParaDon Books, ReadersBooks.info. According to the Great Falls, MT Police Department, the principal, Korede Abayomi, has two arrest warrants in his name.

Infinity Publishing
CAUTION

Ingenium Books

ingeniumbooks.com

RECOMMENDED PARTNER MEMBER

Excellent.

IngramSpark

ingramspark.com

RECOMMENDED PARTNER MEMBER

Excellent.

Inkitt

CAUTION

Aggressive and unprofessional marketing; this service once operated over 40 fake accounts on Twitter to send spam, and was banned from Reddit.

Inkshares

CAUTION

Inkslinger Editing

inkslingerediting.com

RECOMMENDED PARTNER MEMBER

Excellent.

Inkwater

MIXED

Although Inkwater behaves ethically and provides quality work, its pricing precludes our RECOMMENDED rating. Authors are urged to comparison shop.

Inkyeverafterpress

inkyeverafterpress.com

RECOMMENDED PARTNER MEMBER

Excellent.

IPR License
iprlicense.com
Recommended Partner Member
Excellent.

iUniverse
Watchdog Advisory
An Author Solutions vanity press imprint.

I_AM Self-Publishing
iamselfpublishing.com
Recommended Partner Member
Excellent.

JD Smith Design
jdsmith-design.com
Recommended Partner Member
Excellent.

Jenkins Group
Caution

John Hawkins Design
jhbd.co.uk
Recommended

KDP Rocket
kdprocket.com
Recommended

Kindle Direct Publishing (KDP, Amazon)
kdp.amazon.com
Recommended Partner Member
Excellent.

Kindlepreneur (Dave Chesson)
kindlepreneur.com
RECOMMENDED

Kirkus / Kirkus Indie
kirkusreviews.com/indie-reviews
RECOMMENDED
Although Kirkus behaves ethically, the Watchdog Desk has concerns about the value of some aspects of its service, as well as its relationship with Author Solutions.

Kobo
kobo.com/writinglife
RECOMMENDED PARTNER MEMBER
Excellent.

Sarah Kolb-Williams
kolbwilliams.com
RECOMMENDED PARTNER MEMBER
Excellent.

KT Editing (Katherine Trail)
ktediting.com
RECOMMENDED PARTNER MEMBER
Excellent.

Language + Literary Translations
literarytranslations.us
RECOMMENDED PARTNER MEMBER
Excellent.

Lateral Action (Marc McGuinness)
lateralaction.com
RECOMMENDED PARTNER MEMBER
Excellent.

Lawston Design

lawstondesign.com

RECOMMENDED PARTNER MEMBER

Excellent.

Library Cat Editing Services

catrionatroth.blogspot.com/p/editing-services.html

RECOMMENDED PARTNER MEMBER

Excellent.

LifeRich Publishing

WATCHDOG ADVISORY

Reader's Digest imprint outsourced to Author Solutions.

ListenUp Indie

listenupindie.pub

RECOMMENDED PARTNER MEMBER

Excellent.

The Literary Consultancy

literaryconsultancy.co.uk

RECOMMENDED PARTNER MEMBER

Excellent.

LitFire Publishing

CAUTION

Vanity press with connections to Author Solutions employees, and allegations of deceptive practices.

LitRing

litring.com

RECOMMENDED PARTNER MEMBER

Excellent.

Llumina Press / Breezeway Books
CAUTION

Lucy Ridout Editorial Services
lucyridout.co.uk
RECOMMENDED PARTNER MEMBER
Excellent.

Lulu
CAUTION

Luminare Press
luminarepress.com
RECOMMENDED PARTNER MEMBER
Excellent.

Marfa House / Big Bend Productions
CAUTION

Matador Publishing
troubador.co.uk/matador.asp
RECOMMENDED PARTNER MEMBER
Excellent.

Amie McCracken
amiemccracken.com
RECOMMENDED PARTNER MEMBER
Excellent.

Anita D. McClellan Associates
anitamcclellan.com
RECOMMENDED PARTNER MEMBER
Excellent.

Angela McPherson
RECOMMENDED PARTNER MEMBER
Excellent.

megustaescribir
WATCHDOG ADVISORY
Owned by Penguin Random House, outsourced to Author Solutions.

Michael Faulkner Editorial Services
thebluecabin.com/editing
RECOMMENDED PARTNER MEMBER
Excellent.

Michael Terence Publishing (MTP)
mtp.agency
MIXED

Mill City Press
CAUTION

Sarah Monsma
sarahmonsma.com
RECOMMENDED PARTNER MEMBER
Excellent.

Month9Books (Georgia McBride Media Group)
WATCHDOG ADVISORY
Allegations of failure to pay authors, accounting chaos, unprofessional behavior, and at least one lawsuit places this company in our most severe category.

MorainesEdgeBooks.com *Elting*
morainesedgebooks.com
RECOMMENDED PARTNER MEMBER
Excellent.

More Visual (TheBookCoverDesigners.com)
thebookcoverdesigners.com
RECOMMENDED PARTNER MEMBER
Excellent.

MSBuyer.com
CAUTION
Manuscript buyer operating under the initials "DCP." Actual
company name and location are unknown.

My Author Concierge (Maria Connor)
myauthorconcierge.com
RECOMMENDED

My Book Cave
mybookcave.com
RECOMMENDED PARTNER MEMBER
Excellent.

NetGalley
s2.netgalley.com
RECOMMENDED

New Century Publishing
WATCHDOG ADVISORY
This company was the target of legal action by the Indiana Attorney
General and more than 40 authors.

New Writers Interface
newwritersinterface.com
RECOMMENDED

Nielsen ISBN

nielsenisbnstore.com

RECOMMENDED

As with other ISBN registrars, be wary of unnecessary add-on services.

Nikki Busch Editing

nikkibuschediting.com/index.html

RECOMMENDED PARTNER MEMBER

Excellent.

NOOK Press

MIXED

A Novel Connection

CAUTION

Use of this service appears to violate KDP Select's rules on exclusivity.

Novel Publicity

novelpublicity.com

RECOMMENDED PARTNER MEMBER

Excellent.

Novel Thinking

novelthinking.co.uk

RECOMMENDED

Novel Websites

novel-websites.co.uk

RECOMMENDED PARTNER MEMBER

Excellent.

Oak Tree Publishing

CAUTION

One Stop Fiction
onestopfiction.com
RECOMMENDED

OnlineBookClub.org
onlinebookclub.org
MIXED

OodleBooks
oodlebooks.com
RECOMMENDED

Opprimo Marketing
CAUTION

Natasha Orme
natashaorme.com
RECOMMENDED PARTNER MEMBER
Excellent.

Outskirts Press
CAUTION

OverDrive
company.overdrive.com
RECOMMENDED

PageMaster
pagemaster.ca
RECOMMENDED PARTNER MEMBER
Excellent.

Page Publishing
CAUTION
A vanity press with pervasive advertising.

Palibrio
WATCHDOG ADVISORY
An Author Solutions vanity press imprint.

Palmetto Publishing Group
palmettopublishinggroup.com
MIXED

ParaDon Books
WATCHDOG ADVISORY
Also operates Indie Writer Support, ReadersBooks.info. According to the Great Falls, MT Police Department, the principal, Korede Abayomi, has two arrest warrants in his name.

Partridge Africa
WATCHDOG ADVISORY
An Author Solutions vanity press imprint.

Partridge India
WATCHDOG ADVISORY
An Author Solutions vanity press imprint.

Partridge Singapore
WATCHDOG ADVISORY
An Author Solutions vanity press imprint.

Payhip
payhip.com
RECOMMENDED PARTNER MEMBER
Excellent.

Pegasus Elliot Mackenzie Publishers
WATCHDOG ADVISORY

The Pen Factor

penfactor.com

RECOMMENDED PARTNER MEMBER

Excellent.

PeopleSpeak (Sharon Goldinger)

detailsplease.com/peoplespeak

RECOMMENDED

Perfect the Word

perfecttheword.co.uk

RECOMMENDED PARTNER MEMBER

Excellent.

Peters Fraser and Dunlop

petersfraserdunlop.com

RECOMMENDED PARTNER MEMBER

Excellent.

PickFu

pickfu.com

RECOMMENDED

Pix Bee Design

pixbeedesign.com

RECOMMENDED PARTNER MEMBER

Excellent.

Pixel Tweaks Publications

pixeltweakspublications.com

RECOMMENDED PARTNER MEMBER

Excellent.

PJ Boox
pjboox.com
RECOMMENDED

Prepare to Publish
preparetopublish.com
RECOMMENDED PARTNER MEMBER
Excellent.

Print2Demand
print2demand.co.uk
RECOMMENDED PARTNER MEMBER
Excellent.

ProofProfessor (Matt Rance)
WATCHDOG ADVISORY
Complaints about vindictive, bullying, and harassing behavior
warrant extreme caution.

ProWritingAid
prowritingaid.com
RECOMMENDED PARTNER MEMBER
Excellent.

Publica.io
publica.io
RECOMMENDED PARTNER MEMBER
Excellent.
Because blockchain technology is in its infancy, it is difficult to assess
the ramifications of its use. However, Publica.io is reputable and
adheres to ALLi's Code of Standards.

PublishDrive
publishdrive.com
RECOMMENDED PARTNER MEMBER
Excellent.

Published.com
CAUTION

Publish Green
CAUTION

Pubvendo
pubvendo.com
RECOMMENDED PARTNER MEMBER
Excellent.

Raider Publishing
WATCHDOG ADVISORY

Rancho Park Publishing
ranchopark.com
RECOMMENDED

ReadersBooks.info
WATCHDOG ADVISORY
Also operates ParaDon Books, Indie Writer Support. According to the Great Falls, MT Police Department, the principal, Korede Abayomi, has two arrest warrants in his name.

Readers in the Know
readersintheknow.com/home
RECOMMENDED PARTNER MEMBER
Excellent.

Read Out Loud
readoutloud.in
RECOMMENDED

RedheadedBookLover ("Aimee Ann")
CAUTION
In her unsolicited emails, RBL neglects to mention that her reviews are invoiced at $75 each.

 Reedsy
reedsy.com
RECOMMENDED PARTNER MEMBER
Excellent.

 Rethink Press
rethinkpress.com
RECOMMENDED PARTNER MEMBER
Excellent.

Reviewers for Books
CAUTION

Robin Ludwig Design (gobookcoverdesign.com)
gobookcoverdesign.com
RECOMMENDED

Rob Siders (52 Novels)
52novels.com
RECOMMENDED PARTNER MEMBER
Excellent.

Rocket Science Productions / RSP Marketing Services
CAUTION
"Phase One" of this publishing scheme involves a $595 payment for copyright registration and an ISBN.

Sally Vince Editorial Services
editorsal.com
RECOMMENDED PARTNER MEMBER
Excellent.

Scotforth Books
scotforthbooks.com
RECOMMENDED PARTNER MEMBER
Excellent.
Scotforth Books is an imprint of Carnegie Publishing.

Scribd
scribd.com
RECOMMENDED
Scribd has a rocky history with regard to piracy and its subscription services, but these complaints do not extend to its interactions with authors.

Seenapse
seenapse.it
RECOMMENDED

SELF-e
MIXED

SelfPubBookCovers
selfpubbookcovers.com
RECOMMENDED PARTNER MEMBER
Excellent.

Self Publishing Formula (Mark Dawson)
selfpublishingformula.com
RECOMMENDED PARTNER MEMBER
Excellent.

Serious Reading
CAUTION

Shakspeare Editorial
shakspeareeditorial.org
RECOMMENDED PARTNER MEMBER
Excellent.

She Writes Press
MIXED

S & H Publishing
sandhbooks.com
RECOMMENDED PARTNER MEMBER
Excellent.

SilverWood Books
silverwoodbooks.co.uk
RECOMMENDED PARTNER MEMBER
Excellent.

Sleeping Cat Books
sleepingcatbooks.com
RECOMMENDED

Smashwords
smashwords.com
RECOMMENDED PARTNER MEMBER
Excellent.

Society for Editors and Proofreaders (SfEP)
sfep.org.uk
RECOMMENDED PARTNER MEMBER
Excellent.

The Soulful Pen (Carla Wynn Hall)
CAUTION

Standoutbooks
standoutbooks.com
RECOMMENDED PARTNER MEMBER
Excellent.

Stergiou Ltd
stergioultd.com
RECOMMENDED PARTNER MEMBER
Excellent.

Ellie Stevenson
elliestevenson.wordpress.com
RECOMMENDED PARTNER MEMBER
Excellent.

Strategic Book Publishing and Rights Agency (SBPRA, Robert Fletcher)
WATCHDOG ADVISORY
SBPRA has been the subject of legal action compelling it to repay $125,000.00 to authors.

Stratton Press
CAUTION

StreetLib
streetlib.com
RECOMMENDED PARTNER MEMBER
Excellent.

SWATT Books
swatt-books.co.uk
RECOMMENDED PARTNER MEMBER
Excellent.

Sweek.com
sweek.com
RECOMMENDED

Swift Publishing
CAUTION

Swoon Romance (Georgia McBride Media Group)
CAUTION
See Month9Books for additional information.

Tantor Media
tantor.com
RECOMMENDED

Tantrum Books (Georgia McBride Media Group)
CAUTION
See Month9Books for additional information.

Tate Publishing
WATCHDOG ADVISORY
Tate Publishing has been closed since its owners were arrested and charged with multiple felonies.

Terry Gilbert-Fellows (Blackheath Dawn)
blackheathdawn.co.uk
RECOMMENDED PARTNER MEMBER
Excellent.

Thomson-Shore
thomsonshore.com
RECOMMENDED

Tom Evans, Bookwright
tomevans.co
RECOMMENDED PARTNER MEMBER
Excellent.

Trafford Publishing
WATCHDOG ADVISORY
An Author Solutions vanity press imprint.

Upgrade Your Story
upgradeyourstory.com
RECOMMENDED

Vervante
vervante.com
RECOMMENDED PARTNER MEMBER
Excellent.

Voyage Media
CAUTION

WestBow Press
WATCHDOG ADVISORY
Thomas Nelson & Zondervan imprint outsourced to Author Solutions.

Where Writers Win
writerswin.com
RECOMMENDED PARTNER MEMBER
Excellent.

Whitefox Publishing Services
wearewhitefox.com
RECOMMENDED PARTNER MEMBER
Excellent.

The Wishing Shelf Independent Book Awards
thewsa.co.uk
RECOMMENDED PARTNER MEMBER
Excellent.

Woman Safe Health
womansafehealth.com
RECOMMENDED PARTNER MEMBER
Excellent

Wordclay
WATCHDOG ADVISORY
An Author Solutions vanity press imprint.

Woven Red Author Services (Joan Frantschuk)
wovenred.ca
RECOMMENDED PARTNER MEMBER
Excellent.

WriteIndia, aka Times of India
WATCHDOG ADVISORY
Allegations of contract manipulation warrant our WATCHDOG
ADVISORY.

Writers.Support
WATCHDOG ADVISORY
An alias of Crystalline Noble.

Writing.ie

writing.ie
RECOMMENDED PARTNER MEMBER
Excellent.

Writing for Children with Karen Cioffi

karencioffiwritingforchildren.com
RECOMMENDED PARTNER MEMBER
Excellent.

Written Word Media

writtenwordmedia.com
RECOMMENDED PARTNER MEMBER
Excellent.

XinXii

xinxii.com
RECOMMENDED

Xlibris

WATCHDOG ADVISORY
An Author Solutions vanity press imprint.

Xlibris AU

WATCHDOG ADVISORY
An Author Solutions vanity press imprint.

Xlibris NZ

WATCHDOG ADVISORY
An Author Solutions vanity press imprint.

Xlibris UK

WATCHDOG ADVISORY
An Author Solutions vanity press imprint.

Xulon Press
Caution

York Publishing Services
yps-publishing.co.uk
Recommended Partner Member
Excellent.

Your Author Engine
yourauthorengine.com
Recommended Partner Member
Excellent.

PART V

HOW TO EVALUATE SELF-PUBLISHING SERVICES

20

THE RATING PROCESS

To conclude our guide to choosing a self-publishing service, we present guidelines and tools for evaluating any service yourself.

Researching a service may seem overwhelming at first, but take comfort in the fact that industry watchdogs and the company's clients may have already done the bulk of the work for you.

CONSULTING WATCHDOGS

Industry watchdogs like Victoria Strauss of Writer Beware!, David Gaughran, and ALLi review many service providers, big and small. Even if these author advocates haven't performed an in-depth review of the companies you're considering, you may find echoes of their behavior among the reports of scams and substandard services.

However, be aware that all watchdogs are not equal and those outside the self-publishing sector often fail to grasp the issues at stake.

The Better Business Bureau

The Better Business Bureau (BBB) is one glaring example of a consumer watchdog that has failed its mission. The BBB offers paid "accreditation" that places a rating from "A+" to "F" on the provider's listing. The very practice of soliciting money from the providers it is supposed to monitor is troubling. Even more troubling is the fact that providers notorious for their predatory behavior were inexplicably awarded A+ ratings after paying for accreditation.

Despite these ethical and practical concerns, the BBB does have its uses. Consumers often leave reviews and complaints on the BBB website, and if you disregard the BBB's assessment of whether the issue was "resolved" or not, these complaints can offer insights into the customer experience and dangerous patterns of behavior by the service provider.

View positive reviews on the BBB site with skepticism. Few people go out of their way to log on to this website, search for a company, and then post a glowing review. Consumers visit the BBB website for two primary reasons: to gather information, and to complain. Effusive praise is likely posted at the urging of the company, often at a time when a novice author is starry-eyed from the promises of a manipulative sales department and unaware of just how badly they have been exploited.

PERFORMING YOUR OWN EVALUATIONS

With the rapid growth and evolution of the self-publishing industry, the number of providers serving authors has grown as well. At ALLi, we aim to identify many of the worst operators, and shine a spotlight on some of the best author-centric services. However, the volume of new companies surfacing rapidly outpaces any watchdog's ability to review.

Just as indie authors must learn aspects of publishing, distribution, and marketing, so they must also learn to appraise potential service providers to protect themselves from exploitation.

View Provider Websites Critically

A prospective service provider's website is a good place to start your research, but always remember that the website is a marketing tool under the provider's exclusive control, designed to present it in the best possible light. It should be viewed with a healthy dose of skepticism.

However, the *manner* in which that information is presented may prove even more useful than the information itself.

Is the website professionally designed, with well-edited copy? A provider that can't be bothered (or doesn't know how) to present its offering professionally is likely to cut corners on your work as well.

Is information about pricing and services presented clearly, upfront, and without evasion? A provider that doesn't disclose pricing or is vague about the services provided may be trying to conceal vital information from you.

Does the marketing pitch rely on intimidation, or attempt to belittle you or prey on your insecurities? Does it falsely claim that the provider's services are the only path to success? Does it drip with contempt at a particular sector of the publishing industry, either indie or traditional? These are all signs of a company that tears authors down rather than building them up and supporting them.

Examine the Service's Work

If possible, look up examples of the service provider's work. If the company provides cover art, are the designs eye-catching and unique, or are they repetitive templates? If it provides editing, are their books free of errors? If it provides marketing and publicity, is the book easily found outside of the provider's website?

Don't rely on the carefully selected examples spotlighted by the company. These are cherry-picked to show their best work. You'll want to see a random sampling of the work they typically produce, one that includes examples of the good and the potentially bad.

Listen to Your Fellow Authors

When shopping for a service provider, the recommendations of trusted friends and colleagues are invaluable. Each person in your circle of friends is one node in a much, much larger network, so by asking for recommendations, you're not only tapping into their personal experience, but the experiences of their friends and colleagues. Take advantage of the power of that network.

Author groups on social media are another powerful resource. If you're not a member of a group that includes seasoned, professional authors, you're missing out on a priceless source of information.

Seek Out Complaints

It's somewhat counterintuitive, but complaints can be one of the best indicators of a provider's quality of service. As mentioned earlier, glowing reviews may be solicited by the provider itself, or posted by naive clients who are unaware that they're being exploited.

Complaints, on the other hand, are a glimpse behind the polished façade that the provider presents. Watch for the following:

- **Quantity of complaints:** Dissatisfied customers are an inevitable part of doing business. At some point in the lifecycle of any business, something will go wrong, a customer will be unhappy, and they will complain about it online. These isolated negative reviews should not be an automatic disqualifier when evaluating a service provider. However, when the number of complaints is substantial, that suggests a problem with the way that provider is serving its clients.
- **Consistency of complaints:** Watch for recurring themes in complaints, especially issues concerning hidden fees, poor customer service, worthless services, or services not delivered. These patterns may reveal incompetence or predatory behavior. Communication is particularly

important, as predatory providers tend to shower new clients with attention until they've got the client's money in hand. Then the communication abruptly dries up, and the client is relegated to voicemail limbo while the next victim is being courted.

- **Reactions to complaints:** Be on the lookout for threatening, blame-shifting, rude, vindictive, or litigious responses by the provider's representatives. This is a bright red danger sign that signals an abusive, unprofessional operation.

GOOD SIGNS

Companies with a strong track record for pleasing clients tend to share certain characteristics. Be on the lookout for these traits—and note when they are absent.

Information Upfront

A good company website provides information upfront, and in plain, jargon-free English. You shouldn't have to root out information buried in the depths of the site. Providers should clearly and frankly explain what services they provide, how it's done, and what it will cost.

Competitive Pricing

Low cost is always attractive when combined with high quality. As an author starting out, the trick is to aim high, in terms of publishing standards, but to keep your costs to a minimum. A careful and critical assessment of the company's work is key here, as well as comparison shopping.

Realistic Empathy

The provider makes every effort to understand your book, your ambitions, your abilities, and your budget, while also giving you a reality check about commercial viability.

Positive Track Record

There is nothing more valuable than the experience of another author whom you trust. Seek out recommendations and advice from your friends and author community.

If possible, contact some of the authors who have worked with the company to get their firsthand assessment. Although authors may be willing to discuss this in a public forum, they will be far more candid about their experiences and success with a publishing service if you contact them privately and off the record.

Good Team

Staff should be tactful and pleasant. You should get a sense of teamwork, with everyone behind your project.

Author-Friendly, Clear Contract

You should see a formal contract, clearly worded in terms you can understand. The copyright should remain with you, the author; you should not be tied in for any fixed time period or bound to exclusivity. Rights granted should cover only the minimum needed to perform the work.

Contacts and Connections

Where appropriate, the provider should have established relationships within the distribution chain from top to bottom (distributors, wholesalers, retailers, readers) and an online shop. It should also be able, and willing, to direct you to other distribution channels.

No Unreasonable Fees

A lot of money can be made from authors after they publish. One way companies do this is through correction or alteration fees, which means if you find an error in your book and want to change it, you'll have to pay. This is one feature of IngramSpark that we at ALLi don't love, and though we appreciate very much that the company has waived change fees for our members, we look forward to the day all authors can make the changes they need to make without penalty.

Even the best providers charge these fees—but it's how much they charge that separates the good from the bad.

It's worth noting that for some services, such as cover design, correction fees are standard and appropriate. The terms governing these changes should be clearly defined in the agreement or contract.

WARNING BELLS

Substandard companies also tend to have predictable traits. Be on the lookout for these warning signs, and if you see them, be prepared to walk away.

Providers Who Ask for Your Rights and Charge You for Them

There are some publishers who will ask for terms of up to three or five years, plus exclusivity, and charge you fees on top of that.

In the publishing business, an author expects compensation for the rights they give up. This compensation generally comes in the form of a royalty payment on each copy sold, and sometimes an advance on royalties while the book is produced and distributed.

The advance and the royalty are an exchange for the author handing over the right to print, copy, publish, and sell the work.

These are valuable assets, and no provider should ask for them without offering suitable compensation.

Providers Who Act like Car Sales Staff

This is a common occurrence in the self-publishing world, especially with certain package providers. After contacting the provider, an author can be bombarded with emails and phone calls urging authors to publish. In ALLi's opinion, this is poor form. Authors should be given facts and left to decide, not submerged in sales pitches that lack information.

In our experience, this tactic of high-pressure sales is usually practiced by companies whose interests lie with rapid turnover and conveyor-belt-style profit models, rather than those who are invested in supporting the author.

Representatives

Beware the title "representative." In the publishing world, as in many other industries, representatives exist to sell you something. So, if a self-publishing service talks of putting you through to a representative, or "your rep," you may be in for a sales pitch. Be ready to put the phone down and move on if this turns out to be more marketing and hype than useful information about the service.

Vagueness

Providers that offer comprehensive information upfront are the best ones to deal with. When you're trying to decide whether a company can provide what you need at the right price, you don't want to dig through their website or pages of marketing to ferret out information one fragment at a time.

High Prices

Price and value are two distinct metrics, and more expensive doesn't necessarily mean higher quality.

Always assess what you are paying for, and what it will take to recoup. High prices put authors in debt, and it can take years for them to break even, if they ever do. Be value-conscious and crunch the numbers on any prospective purchase.

Hidden Fees

When you know that KDP and Kobo and iBooks charge no service fees, give authors access to so many readers, and provide up to a 70% royalty rate (in the author's favor), it really does put other providers into perspective.

Look deep for costs such as revision charges, annual fees, renewal fees, or down payments. Watch also for low royalties and commissions. With today's technology, there is no excuse for providers masking their own profit with high administration fees or inflated manufacturing costs that all bite into your revenue.

Required Purchases

Publishers should be selling books to readers, not authors. Avoid any publisher with a contractual requirement to purchase copies of your own book. This is a common vanity press tactic used to extract more money from authors.

SPECIAL CONCERNS FOR PUBLISHING SERVICES

It's especially important here to note the difference between a publisher and an assisted publishing service.

While an assisted publishing service is transactional and leaves some of the responsibility for the book in the hands of the author, a publisher has a deeper commitment to and greater responsibility for ensuring the success of the book.

An assisted publishing service sells services to authors. A publisher, however, sells books to readers. Always keep in mind which model you're dealing with.

In addition to compliance with our Code of Standards, there are specific issues we look for when evaluating a potential Partner Member for ALLi, particularly ones that offer publishing services.

Nonexclusive Contract with Clear Terminology

Never sign a contract with a service provider unless you have fully read and understand what you are signing. Some providers issue a physical contract, while others will request a click to a "terms of service" document online.

As an author looking for a service, you should receive a contract that refers to an agreed set of services: some combination of editing, design, formatting, print, distribution, marketing, and promotion. The contract should be nonexclusive, meaning that you can use other companies' services for your book at any time.

You should not be assigning secondary publication rights, copyright, or subsidiary rights (film, TV, translation, etc.) to the provider. These are valuable assets that should not be given away without suitable compensation and careful consideration.

A reputable service will also include a clause outlining the termination of the agreement: by who, when, and how it can be initiated. A termination fee is an immediate red flag in any agreement, and should avoided.

If you start to read the terms of the contract and they appear unclear, or there is an overuse of legal terminology, it may be an indicator that the contract is not author-friendly and was drawn up solely to protect the rights of the provider in the event of legal action.

If you are unsure about the contract or any terms, always request clarification. If your service is cagey about answering direct questions, take your business elsewhere.

Transparent Explanation of Fees and Royalties

Understand whether quoted discounts or royalties on book sales are offered based on the retail price of a book or on the net receipts (the money the service collects).

For example, one hypothetical company offers "80% royalties." Does that mean 80% of the list price, 80% of the sale price, or 80% of net? If your ebook is priced at $6.99, 80% of list price would pay $5.59 per sale.

But let's say it's 80% of net, or rather 80% of what's left over after the retailer takes its share. To your dismay, you might discover that the distributor pays only 35% on each sale, and the publisher then pays you 80% of that, for a final payment of $1.95.

That's quite a difference.

Ascertain what the base cost of printing a book is, and what price the provider charges to offer books directly to you. If it's difficult to elicit this information, then it's likely the provider has something to hide and wishes to confuse and complicate the process.

Markup on author copies can be severe. Avoid publishers who make money selling books to authors rather than readers.

Publishers Focus on Book Sales

The end goal of any publisher is to sell books. Accordingly, a true publisher's website should be focused on books, not on authors or services.

Look for:

- Books prominently displayed on the website
- Professional quality, particularly cover design and interior layout
- Prominent links to retailers or an option to buy
- Evidence of external promotions, such as book launches, signings, and other author events

If these signs are missing from a publisher's website, you may be dealing with an assisted self-publishing service masquerading as a traditional publisher. Be on guard, and investigate further.

Multiformat Availability

Look for a publisher that offers a variety of print formats and distribution platforms. Few services have the resources to print in-house, but they should have external print partnerships or affiliate agreements to meet customer requirements.

If your publisher cannot offer a hardback print edition, an offset print run, an EPUB or MOBI format, or a full-color interior, it's likely they are relying on limited print resources (possibly only a POD facility) and have few or no distribution programs in place.

Ownership of Book Files

If you paid for the editing, formatting, and conversion of your manuscript to a digital format, you should own it. A good self-publishing service provider will make the source files available to you on request so that you can make changes in the future.

A traditional publisher will never ask you to pay for this work, but is also unlikely to provide the source files to you.

Always seek clarity on this key issue before you enter the production process.

Access or Referral to Editing Professionals and Services

A self-publishing service package should offer access to professional editors (named and listed) and any other pre- and post-production services required. If the provider does not offer such information, it may be a clear sign that it accepts anything for production "as is," no matter how poor the quality.

Be wary of a provider that will not give the name of a specific publishing professional or affiliated service it uses.

A good service will always advise you on what work is required to improve your book. You should also be free to work with any other external service or professional you wish in conjunction with your chosen service. If the provider cannot be flexible in this regard, it may be working for its own benefit rather than yours.

ISBN Ownership

A good assisted publishing service will always offer you the option of using your own ISBNs and publishing imprint name. Do not let the provider insist you use its assigned ISBN. By doing this, you give up the right to be identified as the publisher of your book.

There is nothing inherently wrong with using an assigned ISBN from a provider so long as you understand that you, the author, will not be the "publisher of record." As such, you cannot take that edition of your book to another service without first changing the book files and logos and reregistering the new edition with your own ISBN and publishing imprint.

Agreements with Wholesalers and Distributors

It's important as a self-publisher to understand the difference between a wholesaler and a distributor. We covered this distinction in detail in Part V, and it's worth a refresher.

A wholesaler is a company with a warehouse and a vast database of listed books—some physically housed there as well as "available" on a database inventory for purchase and shipment to booksellers.

A distributor has a team of sales representatives operating on behalf of a list of client publishers, dedicated to selling its catalogue of books to buyers in bookstores.

A wholesaler reacts to book orders from the trade, whereas a distributor is proactive about selling its clients' books to the trade. So, a self-publishing service listing books with a wholesaler won't, in and of itself, sell a single book.

Few self-publishing services have book distribution deals in place, despite the claims you may hear. They largely depend on online print book sales through vendors like Amazon and Barnes & Noble, and ebook sales through platforms like Apple's iBookstore and Amazon's Kindle Store—functions you can easily and cheaply organize for yourself.

These are rarely successful in getting print books onto the shelves of physical bookstores, either major chains or independent stores. Those that do succeed achieve it by having small niche distribution deals, often direct, and combined with considerable input and promotion by authors and their social networks. If any provider is promising you this service, read the fine print. Ask how it will deliver this distribution.

Many self-publishing services use Ingram for print (and, since the advent of IngramSpark, for ebooks too), as this gets print books listed in the Ingram book catalogue. Ingram, the largest book wholesaler in the US, also operates as a distributor for many large and independent publishers. In the UK, Gardners is the largest wholesaler of books, and Bertrams is another UK wholesaler offering distribution services.

However hard a service works to support and promote a book, its primary revenue comes from providing solutions to an author's needs. Most providers are not Macmillan or Random House. The best may have the success and penetration of a small independent press, but most are little more than printers.

Strong Presence on Social Networks

Social networking is an important tool in the arsenal of a self-published author. It is fertile ground to grow contacts, reach like-minded people, and promote fan bases and brand following.

It can be a red flag when you don't see a provider on any social network, but it's not necessarily a negative. It might suggest that the provider has limited staff resources; that it doesn't understand the importance of social media; or that it's hiding from public exposure and criticism. If a company's social media presence is scant or missing, dig deeper to find out why.

Transparency of Staff Skills

Too many self-publishing services are opaque about the number of staff members, and about skill sets and experience in publishing, editing, design, and marketing.

This is frequently true of one- or two-person operations, which may present themselves as much more. There is nothing wrong with small operators—which account for some of our most valued Partner Members—as long as there is no misrepresentation or obfuscation. A good service delivers what it promises, and is upfront about what its capabilities are.

To that end, any publisher or assisted self-publisher should be transparent about who is on its staff, and what their experience is.

If the company relies on outside contractors, that should be clearly disclosed, and you must verify who ultimately bears responsibility for the quality of the work.

Communication

Communication is the biggest complaint we hear from authors who contact us about problems with a provider. Whether it's failure to disclose important information or a failure to respond to inquiries in a timely manner, lack of communication erodes trust and creates uncertainty in the author.

Your service should listen to you and identify your needs. Both of you should agree on your book's requirements, and you should never feel that you are being sold services you don't need.

Poor self-publishing services often have high staff turnover because interns or part-timers are employed to fill gaps. Authors are shunted from one person to another, with little satisfaction from anyone. Ask about communication systems and who's in charge if something goes wrong.

As the director of your book's development, you should be in control of the process, and that means understanding at any given moment what's being done, who's doing it, and what the status of that task is.

If your provider doesn't have the ability to work well with you, communicate and update you in a timely fashion, and keep to deadlines, then take your business elsewhere.

21

TEN QUESTIONS TO ASK A SELF-PUBLISHING SERVICE

When choosing a service, find out the answer to these questions before you sign any contract.

1. What Rights Am I Encumbering?

When a right is licensed to another entity, it is *encumbered*; its use becomes restricted by the other party, and potentially less valuable because of that restriction. Understand the consequences of encumbering rights, even if the license you're granting is nonexclusive and time limited. Limit the license to what is appropriate for the payment you are receiving. If you are paying for the service outright, ensure you retain all rights. For more on rights, see our guidebook, *How Authors Sell Publishing Rights*.

2. Where Will My Book Be Distributed and Sold?

Ask for a list. Ask what distribution means in this instance. Will somebody be engaging with booksellers on your behalf, or are you just going to be placed on a database or website along with hundreds of thousands of others, with no discoverability service built in?

3. Is Your Service Exclusive or Nonexclusive?

Digital publishing services marketed directly to authors almost always operate on a nonexclusive basis. That means you can use the service to sell your ebook while simultaneously selling your ebook in other venues.

There are three notable exceptions to this, all big players:

- You need an Apple computer or emulator to create ebooks with Apple's iBooks Author tool. It's a proprietary format.
- Ebooks enrolled in Amazon's optional KDP Select program (which gives better royalty terms in some areas and allows your book to be lent to Amazon Prime readers through Amazon's "library") are exclusive to Amazon for the period of enrollment. This 90-day term of enrollment is renewed automatically unless the author leaves the program.
- Audible, the audiobooks distributor, reduces royalties for those who choose the nonexclusive option.

4. Who Owns the Files after Publication?

ALLi's line on this is simple: If you have paid for conversion and formatting services, you should own the finished files. Steer clear of services that don't facilitate this.

5. Can I Make Changes to My Book after It Goes on Sale?

Most direct retailers like Kobo and KDP allow you to upload new and revised files as often as you like. Smashwords, and Draft2Digital are the only distributors to allow this. Other multichannel distributors, like BookBaby and Ingram, charge fees for every change you make.

6. Do I Set My Own Prices?

While some services have restrictions (e.g. KDP won't allow prices below $0.99), standard practice is to let authors set their own pricing. Amazon also guarantees its customers (readers) that they won't find your book at a lower price elsewhere, so if you reduce your price elsewhere, Amazon may lower the price of your book to match, at its discretion.

Some authors who want to use "permafree" books as a marketing tool use this to their advantage, making their ebook available for free elsewhere, knowing Amazon may then match the price to free. This has proven trickier in recent years, as Amazon has shown increasing reluctance to price match, but it is still a viable strategy.

7. Is Payment an Upfront Fee or a Percentage of Sales or Both?

This is one of the most important clauses in your contract.

Giving up a percentage of sales can ease the financial burden on cash-strapped authors, and ensures that the service provider has an incentive to see your book succeed. However, the cumulative cost of that percentage of sales will likely outweigh the value of the service in the long term.

Paying in advance means you won't have an ongoing deduction from your sales, but requires caution: once the service provider has your money in hand, will it remain dedicated to the success of your book?

The ideal payment arrangement will likely depend on your sales expectations and your immediate budget.

8. How Is My Royalty Calculated?

While different services have different models, the fees should be transparent and upfront. For example:

KDP, Barnes & Noble's NOOK Press, and Apple's iBooks are all free to use until the point of sale. They make their money by taking a cut of each sale, from 30% upwards. This share may increase depending on your pricing.

The Smashwords service is similarly free to use and it distributes to all major ebook retailers except Amazon.

BookBaby and other distributors charge fees upfront. You earn "100 percent net" from these services, but that number can be misleading, as "net" may include several fees and deductions from your sales.

Always read the royalty terms carefully. Many companies are less than transparent in the figures they offer. For example, one service claims to offer free e-publishing services plus 100% royalties, but that's only if the sale is made on its own site. Even then, there's a 30% "bookstore fee." Ultimately, you're receiving 70%, not 100%.

Crunch the numbers. If, like many writers, numbers make your head spin, get somebody to help.

9. Are There Any Extra Fees or Charges I Should Know About?

Are there instances in which you might end up paying more than standard rates for conversion or formatting? For example, if your book is longer than average, if you have a lot of charts, tables, or images requiring formatting, and so on, will you be subject to additional charges? Make sure no questionable items are lurking in the terms of agreement or the contracts. Highlight any potential issues at the quotation stage to avoid unpleasant surprises later in the process.

10. Where's the Value?

Your service provider should be able to explain how it adds value to your book, without excessive hype or grandiose promises, and to point to examples of its successful work. A service provider should do more than simply complete a task you could do yourself, but rather should improve the process, applying unique strengths and assets to your book.

DOs & DONTs
DO:

- Find out how the publishing business works.
- Talk to successful self-published authors.
- Take your time.
- Ignore the provider's own "author testimonials." Instead, contact an author from its bookstore page who is not mentioned in a testimonial.
- Know all your options.
- Evaluate quality. Order a couple of the service's books in the format you're planning to use, so you can assess physical quality and order fulfillment.
- Investigate reputations. Do a web search on the service's name plus "complaint" and "scam."
- Buy your own ISBNs directly from your regional registrar.
- Refer to reliable and established writing organizations and bodies such as your local writers' representative body, ALLi, Writer Beware!, and the Independent Publishing Magazine.
- Follow ALLi's Self-Publishing Advice Blog and those of our trusted advisors, such as Joel Friedlander, Joanna Penn, and Jane Friedman.
- Look for flexibility and a best match for your needs.
- Compare services and pricing.
- Look carefully at any contracts and terms of service. If considering an assisted service, choose one that offers all formats, nonexclusivity, and doesn't push add-ons.
- Know your own creative intentions, and be realistic.

DON'T:

- Open your wallet until you are sure the publishing step you're about to take is the right one for you and your book.

- Be rushed into a decision; reject high-pressure sales tactics and limited-time offers.
- Assume or take things on trust.
- Restrict yourself to what you find through Google searches.
- Accept the first provider you find.
- Purchase rigid, all-in-one packages that contain services you don't need or want.
- Choose a print-on-demand provider without understanding the limitations of POD technology.
- Pay your POD publishers hefty fees for Kindle and/or iPad conversions as an additional fee-based service.
- Choose a self-publishing service that pretends to be a trade-publisher, or pretends it can do more for your book than is actually possible.
- Think you're "published" by Simon & Schuster or other traditional publishers if you are paying for it.
- Rely on online testimonials and company sales reps.
- Sign anything without reading the fine print.
- Pay before understanding what services you are getting.

22

ALLI CODE OF STANDARDS

I n the previous chapter, we rated hundreds of self-publishing services and vendors. These ratings (more easily searched on our website), offer a means of swiftly weeding out bad operators and identifying the good ones.

All ALLi's Partner Members must agree to adhere to our Code of Standards. The Code is our guidepost and your first line of defense against unscrupulous operators.

Services that adhere to the principles of our **Code of Standards** are likely to offer a positive experience to their clients. Services that fail to live up to these standards do not have the author's best interests at heart.

Integrity

We recognize that Partner Membership of ALLi means our primary aim is to enable authors to effectively publish and sell books. We follow through on all promised services and fully honor all advertisements and publication agreement terms. We never spam, oversell, harass authors to buy our services, or sell a dream to the uninitiated.

Integrity is the most critical aspect of a client–vendor relationship, and it's often the hardest one to evaluate. Companies may offer much, but once the contract is signed and the client's payment is in hand, they may fail to deliver on their promises.

This is where customer reviews prove to be a precious source of information, especially word of mouth from trusted colleagues. If you're relying on anonymous customer reviews, view them with restraint. Whether named or anonymous, while one negative review may be a fluke, an impossible-to-please client, or even someone with a personal grudge, numerous complaints from multiple sources indicate a pervasive problem.

Services that rely on spam, high-pressure sales tactics, or inflated promises should also be regarded with caution. These are the hallmarks of trying to find a client for a product, rather than trying to find the right service for the client. Integrity demands that the service provider works to the benefit of the author. One that's more concerned with meeting a sales quota than with serving your needs has abandoned that principle.

Value

We add value to each publication commensurate with the fee charged, relieving authors of key publishing tasks, enhancing readability, design, or discoverability.

Price and value are related but separate issues. One provider may have reasonable pricing, but still deliver poor value, either failing to honor promises made or bringing useless services that don't benefit the author. Another may have higher-than-average pricing but deliver exceptional value for that fee. (Don't assume that higher pricing means better service, however. In the majority of cases, it does not.)

The best way to appraise the value of a service is to examine the end result. If it's providing editing, are clients' books well edited? If it's publishing to retailers, are the sales pages professional and error-free? If the provider specializes in marketing and publicity, can you see evidence of their footprint on the landscape of the internet?

When the results of the service are not easily gauged, as with certain PR services, customer reviews are again a useful guide. If the typical customer is disappointed with the results, chances are you will be too.

Clarity

We make clear what we can and cannot do for the self-publishing writer and how our service compares to others.

Service providers must be clear about what services they are providing, and how those services will benefit the author. Too many self-publishing services rely on vague descriptions of services and even more vague promises of success. This can lead to confusion and open the door to deceptive practices.

When evaluating a provider, learn to slice through the marketing fluff and look for concrete statements about how it operates. If you can't find any, or the provider seems evasive about the process, that's a danger sign.

Examples of Concrete Statements:

- "We distribute your book through Amazon, Barnes & Noble, Apple, and Google Play, and internationally through Ingram's global network."
- "We guarantee 1,000 hits to your Amazon sales page, independently tracked, or your money back."
- "Our Silver Package includes professional cover design and copyediting up to 70,000 words."

Examples of Meaningless Fluff:

- "We distribute your book worldwide." (To what countries? Through what networks?)

- "We will promote your book to our thousands of Facebook and Twitter followers." (How many? Do those followers actually see and interact with the page? Are those followers interested in a book like yours, or are they just other authors promoting their own books?)
- "We take care of everything!" (What, exactly, and how?)

Pricing

Our price quotations are accurate, transparent, and complete. Pricing is in line with market norms.

Pricing should be clearly and fully disclosed, with no hidden fees. Reputable service providers inform their clients; they do not hide vital information from them, especially key information like pricing.

Pricing that is drastically different from market norms—above or below typical pricing—is another red flag. Grossly inflated pricing is rarely justified by the quality of the services rendered. In the other direction, pricing that seems too good to be true usually is.

When comparing prices to determine the market norms, be sure to measure against known, reputable providers with a proven track record. Predatory operators often have higher visibility than the legitimate ones, so comparing the first results you find on Google may yield highly inflated averages.

Partnership

We involve authors in planning and decision-making for key aspects of the publication process, from titles and cover design to sales and marketing strategies.

ALLi characterizes indie authors as creative directors of their books who expect that status to be reflected in any partnership.

Service providers that respect indie authors recognize their role in supporting the author's creative vision. That attitude tends to shine through in their marketing materials and direct communications: "How can we help you succeed?" as opposed to "You need our services." "Here's what we offer," rather than "This is what you need to do."

After the contract is signed, the author should remain an active participant, not a helpless passenger.

Service

We are accountable for our work. We keep authors informed each step of the way and provide good customer service and follow-up.

Good service incorporates all of the other principles in the Code of Standards, but centers on one key concept: accountability. Accountable providers' representatives treat the client as their personal responsibility. They treat the client as a person and not a commodity or case number. When a problem arises, they take steps to correct it, and they follow up to ensure that the client is happy.

But service is most obvious when it's missing. That lack of accountability ripples through every aspect of a provider's operation and every item in the Code of Standards, so those with poor service tend to be flooded with a wide variety of complaints.

Communication

We provide helpful and timely information to authors at all stages of publication, and beyond, and facilitate authors to get any ancillary information we cannot provide.

Communication overlaps with several of the principles in the Code of Standards because it's paramount at all stages of the author–vendor relationship. Correspondingly, it's one of the most common reasons for customer dissatisfaction.

Poor communication can stem from several causes. The vendor might be understaffed and too busy to answer questions. They might not respect the client. Or they might be actively concealing information.

Each of these is a recipe for a disastrous business relationship. If you see complaints about a provider's communication, be wary, particularly if the breakdown seems to happen after the contract is signed.

Remember: You have a right to full and accurate information from a prospective service provider before you enter into any agreement. Pricing, options, and process should all be discussed openly, and these discussions should never be conditional on signing the contract.

You have a right to know what's in the contract you're signing, in clear, easily understood language. Ask to see a typical contract before entering into negotiations. Any unpleasant surprises buried in the contract are a bright red flag that should put you on highest alert.

You have a right to know how your money is being spent, and what actions are being taken on your behalf. When a service provider condescends to a client by saying, "Just let us do our thing," or "It's complicated," it is no longer treating the author as a partner and an equal.

You have a right to regular, timely updates on a project's status. Lack of communication in this area is a frequent cause of customer dissatisfaction—and with good reason.

Community

We have a long-term commitment to author-publishing and support the empowerment of self-publishing authors.

Most reputable service providers are active within the author communities they serve. They show their support for indie authors by catering to the specific needs of self-publishers, by listening to authors, and by joining and supporting professional groups.

However, some providers position themselves in opposition to a community. They pander to disgruntled authors by proclaiming contempt for traditional publishing or prey on insecurities by insisting that authors can't succeed without their help.

Neither attitude reflects the reality of indie authors. No author exists in a vacuum. We are all part of the publishing industry, a larger community that includes self-publishers, traditionally published authors, hybrid authors, service providers, professional organizations, and more.

A service provider that relies on needlessly divisive tactics is not working to empower authors, but rather to isolate them. A service provider that employs this type of manipulation should be viewed with caution.

23

CONCLUSION

You are now equipped to evaluate any self-publishing service but if you run into any trouble at all, we are here to help.

If you have a query or some feedback you'd like to give about a self-publishing service, or if you would like to further discuss any point in this book, write to me at any time:

john@allianceindependentauthors.org

If you're a member don't forget to check out our searchable database in the member zone and to download our Partner Member Directory.

We hope we have helped you to find the perfect service to match your needs at this stage in the growth of your author business.

THE END

MORE ADVICE &
FEEDBACK

SELF-PUBLISHING ADVICE CENTER

The Self-publishing Advice Center is ALLi's outreach service to the wider indie author community. It includes a daily blog, weekly podcast, ratings of self-publishing services, awards and competitions — and you can also buy our other guidebooks there. We'd love to send you a weekly roundup of self-publishing advice from our award-winning blog.

Sign up here for the best tips and tools from the Alliance of Independent Authors

SelfPublishingAdvice.org/roundup

FREE BOOK FOR YOU
SELF-PUBLISHING GLOSSARY

ould you like a free guide to the terms used in this book and in indie publishing? Our glossary explains all the terms an indie author is ever likely to need.

Sign up:
AllianceIndependentAuthors.org/glossary

REVIEW REQUEST

I f you enjoyed this book, would you consider leaving a brief review online on your favorite online bookstore that takes reviews (see below)? A good review is very important to authors these days as it helps other readers know this is a book worth their time.

It doesn't have to be long or detailed. Just a sentence saying what you enjoyed and a star-rating is all that's needed. Many thanks.

C lick to go to store

ACKNOWLEDGMENTS

Thanks are due to many people for the creation of this book. For book production, thanks to Margaret Hunter at Daisy Editorial for editorial and formatting, to Amron Gavron at Wild Clover Book Services for the index, especially for doing it over twice when we made some last minute changes, and to publishing assistant Sarah Begley.

Thanks also to the fine folks at Scrivener for their writing software and Vellum for their formatting app.

In gathering information about self-publishing services, many thanks are due to author community activists like Dan Holloway, David Gaughran, Giacomo (Jim) Giammatteo, Joanna Penn, Mick Rooney, Helen Sedwick, Victoria Strauss and Mark Williams for their unfailing work on behalf of authors.

And, as ever, our thanks to the members of the Alliance of Independent Authors—author and partner members—whose experiences and feedback form the backbone of this book and all ALLi services.

ABOUT THE AUTHOR

From the sunny California beaches where he washed ashore in 2008, John Doppler scrawls tales of science fiction, urban fantasy, and horror—and investigates self-publishing services as the Alliance of Independent Authors' Watchdog. John enjoys helping authors turn new opportunities into their bread and butter. He shares his lifelong passion for all things weird and wonderful on *The John Doppler Effect*: johndopp.com

 facebook.com/johndopp

ABOUT ALLI

ALLi, the Alliance of Independent Authors is the global association
for self-publishing indie authors.

Join us for reliable advice and advocacy,
discounts, free guidebooks and resources, member forums, contract
review, motivation, education and support from a wonderful indie
author community.

AllianceIndependentAuthors.org

facebook.com/AllianceIndieAuthors
twitter.com/indieauthoralli

INDEX

1106 Design, 125

Abbott Press, 115, 125, 126
Abraham, Eleanor, 125
accounting, 110, 117, 118
ACX, 64
add-on packaged services, 106–7
Adirondack Editing, 125
advanced review copies (ARCs), 81
advertising, 86–91
See also marketing services
Aegitas, 125
aggregators, 69, 70
See also distribution
AIA Editing and Publishing, 125
Alison's Editing Service, 125
Alliance of Independent Authors (ALLi), 9–10
Code of Standards, 10, 115, 121–22, 173–78
on comparing service providers, 37
Self-Publishing Advice Centre, 37, 88

Alliant Press, 126

Amazon

ACX, 64

Amazon Giveaway, 91

Amazon Marketing Services (AMS), 70, 87

book listings on, 8, 66, 96, 191

Expanded Distribution program, 70–71

Look Inside the Book feature, 109–10

See also Kindle Direct Publishing (KDP)

America Star Books, 126

Amolibros, 126

Anita D. McClellan Associates, 150

Anthemion Software, 60, 126

Apple

iBooks, 7, 8, 10, 28, 99, 126, 195

iTunes, 70

appraisal of manuscript, 47, 50, 52

Archway Publishing, 26, 115, 126

ARCs (advanced review copies), 81

Areo Books, 126

Atlas Books, 126

audiobooks

production of, 64–65

rights licensing of, 93

royalties of, 195

Author Accelerator, 127

Author Connections, 127

Author Design Studio, 127

AuthorHouse UK, 115, 128

AuthorHouse US, 26, 115, 128, 129

Authoright, 128

Author-ity Authors, 127

Author Learning Center, 128

Author Marketing Club, 128

Author Marketing Experts, 128

author pages, 79, 111

The Author Site, 128

Author Solutions (ASI), 30, 75, 76, 114–15, 128

Author's Republic, 64, 127

Autocrit, 128

award programs, 110

Baggott, Helen, 129

Bakerview Consulting, 129

Balboa Press, 26, 115, 129

Balboa Press UK, 129

BAM! Publish, 129

banner ads, 87

Barbara Bauer Literacy Agency, 129

Barber, Tim, 139

barcodes, 67

See also ISBNs

Bargain Booksy, 88, 129

Barnes & Noble, 27, 70, 175, 191, 196, 217

See also NOOK Press

BB EBooks, 129

Bell, Jessica, 130

Berge Design, 130

BetaBooks, 130

Better Business Bureau (BBB), 179–80

Better Scribe, 130

BiblioBoard, 75

Bibliotheca, 72, 74

Big Bend Productions, 149

Birks Branding & Design, Katie, 130

Blackheath Dawn, 162

Black Rose Writing, 130

Blank Slate Communication, 130

Blasty, 131

Blissetts, 131

Bluebird Consulting, 131

BlueInk Review, 81, 131

Bluewave Publishing, 131

Blurb, 131

BookBaby, 131

Book Barbarian, 88

BookBlast, 132

BookBlastPro, 132

BookBub, 87–88, 132

Book Country, 132

Book Cover Cafe, 132

TheBookCoverDesigners.com, 151

Book Cover Express, 132

Book Create Service, 132

The Book Designer, 133

book doctoring process, 50

book doctors, 52

book files, 57, 189–90, 195

BookFunnel, 133

BookGarage, 133

Book Industry Communication (BIC), 133

book industry overview, 5–8

BookLocker, 133

Bookmasters, 133

Book Nanny, 133

Bookouture, 133

book pricing, 57–58, 122

Bookprinting.com, 133

book promotions, 77, 79, 85, 86, 91, 189

BookPublishing.com, 134

Book Reality, 134

Bookrix, 134

BookRunes, 134

Books-A-Million, 129

Books Butterfly, 134

BookSends, 88
BooksGoSocial, 90, 134
The Books Machine, 134
BooksOnline.best, 135
BooksOnline.directory, 134
Booktango, 135
Bookupy, 135
BookVenture, 135
Bookwright, 163
Bowker, 67, 135
See also ISBNs
Breezeway Books, 135, 149
brick-and-mortar stores, 63, 68, 71–72
Buchanan, Averill, 135
burden of risk in publishing, 65, 117–18
Busch, Nikki, 152
Buzbooks.com, 136

Caliburn Press, 136
Carlton, Dixie Maria, 127
catalogues, 67, 92, 108–9, 191
categories, 27
Chanticleer Book Reviews, 81, 136
Chesson, Dave, 147
Choosy Bookworm, 136
Cioffi-Ventrice, Karen, 136, 165
Clays, 136
Clink Street Publishing, 136
Clio Editing Service, 136
cloudLibrary, 74
coaching, 46–47
Code of Standards (ALLi), 10, 115, 121–22, 173–78
See also Alliance of Independent Authors (ALLi)
Coinlea Services, 137
Coker, Mark, 76

Combined Book Exhibit, 95
communication with service providers, 177–78
Completely Novel, 137
Connor, Maria, 151
Conscious Care Publishing, 137
content editing, 50, 52
contests, book award, 10, 35, 82–84
contracts, 8, 17, 32–33, 34
control, value of, 25–28
conversion services, 59–60
Conway, Jason, 137
copyediting, 51
copyright, 59, 94, 95–98, 107
See also licensing rights
cover design, 55–59
See also design services
Cre8urbrand, 137
CreateSpace. *See* Kindle Direct Publishing (KDP)
CreateThinkDo, 137
CreativeDesignersWriters.com, 137
The Creative Penn, 137
Creativia, 137
Crystalline Noble, 138
customer reviews, 80–81

Daisy Editorial, 138
Damonza.com, 138
Daniel Goldsmith Associates, 138
DartFrog Books, 138
databases, 10, 92
Dawson, Mark, 87, 89, 138, 159
DCP, 138
DeFilippo, Michele, 125
Design for Writers, 139
design services

cover design, 55–59
designer selection, 56–57
do-it-yourself, 58, 61
for formatting, 60–61
identify your needs, 56
legal considerations of, 59
manuscript conversion, 59–60
pricing of, 57–58
source files from, 57
technical considerations, 56
versatility, 57
developmental editing, 50–51
Dick Margulis Creative Services, 139
discounted books, 84–85
Dissect Designs, 139
distribution
about, 68–69, 76
by aggregators, 69
agreements with, 188, 191–92
to brick-and-mortar stores, 71–72
ebook networks for, 69–70
to libraries, 72–73
to online retailers, 70–71
through ebook systems, 73–76
Dog Ear Publishing, 139
do-it-yourself services
cover design, 58
formatting, 61
marketing, 99
Dorrance Publishing, 139
Doyle, Libby, 139
Draft2Digital, 8, 28, 59, 73, 115, 139
D'Souza, Katharine, 139
Dunning-Kruger effect, 46

eBook Dynasty, 140
Ebook Launch, 140
eBook Partnership, 140
ebooks
discovery services for, 75, 87–88
distribution networks for, 69–70
formatting of, 60
systems for, 73–76
eBooksAreForever, 140
Ebooks Cover Design, 140
editing *vs.* self-editing, 50
Editorial.ie, 140
editorial reviews, 81–82
editorial services
access to, 190
book doctors, 52
copyediting/line editing, 51
developmental/content editing, 50–51
editing and self-editing, 50
editor selection, 52–54
proofreading, 51
editor selection, 52–54
Elly Donovan PR, 140
evaluations of service providers, 180–93, 197
Evans, Tom, 163
exclusive *vs.* nonexclusive services, 187–88, 195

Facebook, 88–89, 90, 111
Fairhill Publishing LLC, 139
FastPencil, 140
FCM Publishing, 141
fee transparency, 83, 112, 176, 188, 196–97
FicFun, 141
Fiction Feedback, 141
Findaway Voices, 64

FindPublishingHelp.com, 141
Fingerpress Ltd, 141
First Edition Design Publishing, 141
52 Novels, 158
Five Rainbows, 141
Fletcher, Robert, 161
Foreword Reviews, 81
Formatting Experts (business), 141
formatting services, 60–61
Frantschuk, Joan, 164
free books, 84–85, 91, 109
FreeBooksy, 142
Friedlander, Joel, 133
Fulton Books, 142
Fussy Librarian, 88, 142

GABAL Global Editions, 142
Gardners, 191
Gatekeeper Press, 142
Gaughran, David, 9, 115, 179
genre considerations, 46, 53
Georgia McBride Media Group, 151, 162
Get Published! LLC, 142
GetPublishingHelp.com, 142
ghostwriting, 48
Giammatteo, Jim, 9, 115
Gilbert-Fellows, Terry, 162
Girl Friday Productions, 142
giveaways, book, 86, 91
Goldinger, Sharon, 155
Goodreads Giveaway, 91
Google
Ads, 16, 87, 89
Preview, 109–10
Grammarly, 143

Green Ivy Publishing, 143
Guaranteed Author, 143
Gunboss Books, 143

Hall, Carla Wynn, 144, 161
Happy Self Publishing, 143
Heddon Publishing, 143
Hellgate Press, 143
Hemingway Editor, 143
Hillcrest Media Group / Hillcrest Publishing Group, 143
Hobthross Ltd, 144
Hoffelder, Nate, 115
Hot Pink Publishing, 144
hybrid publishing services, 19, 103–4, 116–18

I_AM Self-Publishing, 146
iBooks, 7, 8, 10, 28, 99, 126, 195
Independent Author Network, 144
Independent Ink, 144
Indie Authors World, 144
IndieBookLauncher, 144
Indie Writer Support, 145
Infinity Publishing, 145
Ingenium Books, 145
IngramSpark, 7, 63, 70–71, 115, 145
Inkitt, 145
Inkshares, 145
Inkslinger Editing, 145
Inkwater, 146
Inkyeverafterpress, 146
IPR License, 146
ISBNs, 66–67, 190
iTunes, 70
iUniverse, 26, 115, 146

JD Smith Design, 146
Jenkins Group, 134, 146
John Hawkins Design, 146

Kindle Direct Publishing (KDP)
book listings and, 27
bookstore of, 191
KDP Rocket, 147
manuscript conversion services, 59
online forums on, 37
POD service, 59
Select Promotional Tools, 91
service ratings of, 147
See also Amazon
Kindlepreneur, 147
KingSumo, 91
Kirkus / Kirkus Indie, 81, 108, 111–12, 147
Kobo, 7, 28, 70, 73, 99, 147
Kolb-Willliams, Sarah, 147
KT Editing, 147

Language + Literary Translations, 148
Lateral Action, 148
Lawston Design, 148
LCCN (Library of Congress Control Number), 107
legal considerations of design services, 59
See also licensing rights
Libby (app), 73
libraries, 72–76
Library Cat Editing Services, 148
Library Journal, 75
licensing rights, 93–99, 194
See also copyright
LifeRich Publishing, 115, 148
line editing, 51

ListenUp Audio, 64
ListenUp Indie, 148
The Literary Consultancy, 148
LitFire Publishing, 149
LitRing, 149
Llumina Press, 135, 149
Lucy Ridout Editorial Services, 149
Lulu, 149
Luminare Press, 149

Macauley, Austin, 127
manuscript appraisal, 28, 47, 50, 52
manuscript conversion, 59–60
Marfa House, 149
marketing services
advertising, 86–91
author pages, 79, 111
book promotions, 91
control of, 25–26, 28
do-it-yourself, 99
effectiveness of, 77–78
good marketing for support, 78
know your own strengths and weaknesses, 79
measuring success with, 92
press releases, 91, 107–8
public relations, 79–80, 109
uncertain results with, 85
Matador Publishing, 19, 73, 149
McClellan, Anita D., 150
McCracken, Amie, 150
McGuinness, Marc, 148
McPherson, Angela, 150
megustaescribir, 150
mentoring, 46–47
metadata, 8, 66, 67

Michael Faulkner Editorial Services, 150
Michael Terence Publishing (MTP), 150
Mill City Press, 150
Monsma, Sarah, 150
Month9Books, 151
MorainesEdgeBooks.com, 151
More Visual, 151
MSBuyer.com, 151
multiformat availability, 189
My Author Concierge, 151
My Book Cave, 151

NetGalley, 73, 151
New Century Publishing, 152
New Writers Interface, 152
Nielsen Book, 67, 152
See also ISBNs
Nikki Busch Editing, 152
NOOK Press, 152, 196
See also Barnes & Noble
A Novel Connection, 152
Novel Publicity, 152
Novel Thinking, 152
Novel Websites, 153

Oak Tree Publishing, 153
offset printing, 63–64
One Stop Fiction, 153
OnlineBookClub.org, 153
online catalogues and databases, 92
See also catalogues; databases
online retailers, 70–71
See also *specific company names*
OodleBooks, 153
Opening Up to Indie Authors (ALLi), 72

Opprimo Marketing, 153
Orme, Natasha, 153
Outskirts Press, 153
OverDrive, 72, 73, 153

packaged services, 105–6
accounting by, 110
add-on services, 106–7
author pages by, 111
awards and recognition programs by, 110
copyright and LCCN registration by, 107
editorial reviews by, 111–12
fees for, 112
free copies by, 109
hybrid publishing, 19, 103–4, 116–18
inclusion in catalogues, 108
for press releases, 107–8
proofs by, 110
publicity and PR in, 109
retailer previews by, 109–10
social media promotion by, 110–11
value of, 22–24
vanity presses, 7, 11, 86, 127–29
See also service providers
PageMaster, 154
Page Publishing, 154
Palibrio, 115, 154
Palmetto Publishing Group, 154
ParaDon Books, 154
Partridge Africa, 154
Partridge India, 154
Partridge Singapore, 154
Payhip, 155
payment, 65, 117, 188–89, 196
Pegasus Elliot Mackenzie Publishers, 155

The Pen Factor, 155

Penguin Random House, 17, 115, 150, 203

Penn, Joanna (The Creative Penn), 9, 137, 198

PeopleSpeak, 155

Perfect the Word, 155

Peters Fraser and Dunlop, 155

PickFu, 155

piracy, 96–97

Pix Bee Design, 155

Pixel Tweaks Publications, 156

PJ Boox, 156

POD services, 59, 189, 198–99

PR. *See* public relations (PR)

Prepare to Publish, 156

press releases, 89–90, 91, 107–8

pricing design services, 57–58

Print2Demand, 156

print-on-demand (POD) production services, 59, 189, 198–99

production services

for audiobooks, 64–65

metadata for, 66–67

offset and specialty, 63–64

payment for, 65

for print books, 62

print-on-demand, 63

promotion. *See* marketing services

proof copies, 110

ProofProfessor, 156

proofreading, 51

ProWritingAid, 156

Publica.io, 156

publicity campaigns, 109

See also marketing services

public relations (PR), 79–80, 109

PublishDrive, 8, 59, 73, 115, 157

Published.com, 157
Publisher's Weekly (PW), 95, 108
Publish Green, 157
PubMatch, 95
Pubvendo, 157

Rafflecopter, 91
Raider Publishing, 157
Rance, Matt, 156
Rancho Park Publishing, 157
ReadersBooks.info, 157
Readers in the Know, 157
Read Out Loud, 158
recognition programs, 110
Redheaded Book Lover, "Aimee Ann," 158
Reedsy, 158
retailer previews, 109–10
Rethink Press, 158
Reviewers for Books, 158
reviews, 80–82, 111–12
rights licensing, 93–99, 194
    See also copyright
Robin Ludwig Design, 158
Rocket Science Productions, 158
Rooney, Mick, 9, 115
royalties, 6–7, 115, 185, 186, 188
R.R. Bowker, 67, 135
    See also ISBNs
RSP Marketing Services, 158

Sally Vince Editorial Services, 159
Scotforth Books, 159
Scribd, 159
Scrivener, 60, 61
Sedwick, Helen, 9, 59, 99

Seenapse, 159

SELF-e, 72, 74–75, 159

self-editing, 50

See also editorial services

SelfPubBookCovers, 159

The Self-Publisher's Legal Handbook (Sedwick), 59

Self-Publishing Advice Centre (ALLi), 37, 88

Self Publishing Formula, 87, 89, 159

Serious Reading, 160

service providers

on book sales, 189

communication of, 193

contracts of, 187

dos and donts with, 197–99

evaluations of, 29–31, 121–22, 180–83, 197

fees and royalties for, 188, 196–97

questions to ask potential, 194–97

researching, 179–80

signs of bad, 185–87

signs of good, 183–85

transparency of, 192

for writing support, 45–48

See also *specific types of services*

Shakspeare Editorial, 160

She Writes Press, 160

Shiel, Lisa A., 141

S & H Publishing, 160

Siders, Rob, 158

SilverWood Books, 160

Sleeping Cat Books, 160

Smashwords, 28, 73, 160

social media broadcasting, 89–90

social networking, 191, 192

Society for Editors and Proofreaders (SfEP), 160

The Soulful Pen, 161

source files, 57, 189–90
specialty printing production, 63–64
Standoutbooks, 161
Stergiou Ltd, 161
Stevenson, Ellie, 161
St. John, Leigh, 143
Strategic Book Publishing and Rights Agency (SBPRA), 161
Stratton Press, 161
Strauss, Victoria, 9, 115, 179
StreetLib, 59, 115, 161
structural editing, 50, 52
subsidiary rights, 94, 188
See also licensing rights
substantive editing, 50–51
SWATT Books, 161
Sweek.com, 162
Swift Publishing, 162
Swoon Romance, 162

Tantor Media, 162
Tantrum Books, 162
Tate Publishing, 162
technical considerations to design, 56, 58
Thomson-Shore, 174
Times of India, 175
trade publishing *vs.* self-publishing, 8–9
Trafford Publishing, 26, 115, 163
Trail, Katherine, 147

Upgrade Your Story, 163
US Copyright Office, 95–96

vanity presses, 7, 18, 25–26, 113–15
Vellum, 60
versatility, 57

Vervante, 163
Vince, Sally, 159
Voyage Media, 163

WestBow Press, 26, 115, 163
Where Writers Win, 163
Whitefox Publishing Services, 163
wholesale agreements, 191–92
The Wishing Shelf Independent Book Awards, 164
Woman Safe Health, 164
Wordclay, 164
Woven Red Author Services, 164
WriteIndia, 164
Writer Beware! (organization), 9, 31, 35, 37, 198
Writers.Support, 164
Writing for Children with Karen Cioffi, 136, 165
Writing.ie, 164
writing services, 45–48
Written Word Media, 142, 165

XinXii, 165
Xlibris, 26, 115, 165
Xlibris AU, 165
Xlibris NZ, 165
Xlibris UK, 165
Xulon Press, 165

York Publishing Services, 166
Your Author Engine, 166

ISBNs
EBOOK: 978-1-909888-91-3
POD SOFTBACK: 978-1-913588-61-8
POD HARDBACK: 978-1-913588-63-2
LARGE PRINT - 978-1-913588-62-5
AUDIO - 978-1-913349-05-9

EDITORIAL: MARGARET HUNTER AT DAISY EDITORIAL
FORMATTING AND INTERIOR DESIGN: MARGARET HUNTER AT DAISY EDITORIAL
INDEX: AMRON GAVRON AT WILD CLOVER BOOK SERVICES
DESIGN: JANE DIXON SMITH

Font Publications is the publishing imprint
for Orna Ross publications
and the Alliance of Independent Authors.

All Font books—fiction, non-fiction and poetry—have the same intention at
source:
to inspire creative independence, emotional freedom and imaginative
connection.

RIGHTS & Other Enquiries: info@ornaross.com

Made in the USA
Columbia, SC
04 January 2022

53395915R00135